MONTFORT UNIVERSITY
CATTHORPE CAMPUS

Telephone (01400 72521

to be returned before the last date stamped

book's are for after this date.

PC898

withdrawn

THE CANINE GOOD CITIZEN

Every Dog Can Be One

THE CANINE GOOD CITIZEN

Every Dog Can Be One

Jack and Wendy Volhard

Illustrations by Melissa Bartlett

HOWELL BOOK HOUSE
New York

Howell Book House
A Prentice Hall Macmillan Company
15 Columbus Circle
New York, NY 10023

Library of Congress Cataloging-in-Publication Data
Volhard, Joachim.
   The canine good citizen, every dog can be one / by Jack and Wendy
Volhard ; illustrations by Melissa Bartlett.
      p.   cm.
   ISBN 0-87605-420-3
   1. Dogs—Training.   2. Dogs—Behavior.   I. Volhard, Wendy.
II. Title.
SF431.V625   1994
636.7′0887—dc20   94-8777
                                                               CIP

Manufactured in the United States of America

10 9 8 7 6 5 4 3 2

In memory of
Can. OTCh. Seaward's C-Pink of Rivendell, UD, VB
(Pinky),
1/3/80–11/30/93,
the ultimate Canine Good Citizen

Contents

The authors giving a two-day seminar for the Nashville Dog Training Club
Photo by Marty Cavanaugh

About the Authors

THE VOLHARDS share their home in upstate New York with eight dogs and four cats. For the past twenty-five years they have taught over 10,000 people how to communicate effectively with their pets. They conduct weekend seminars in various parts of the United States, Canada and England, as well as five-day training camps, which have been attended by individuals from almost every state, Argentina, Australia, Canada, England, Germany, Mexico, the Netherlands, Puerto Rico, the Republic of Singapore and the West Indies. Over the years they have served different dog organizations in a variety of capacities, and are internationally known as "trainers of trainers."

Jack has authored over 100 articles for various dog publications and is the recipient of five awards from the Dog Writers' Association of America (DWAA). He is the senior author of four books and four videotapes. He has been an AKC judge since 1973, is approved for all Obedience classes and is a member of the Association of Dog Obedience Clubs and Judges.

Wendy is the recipient of three awards from the DWAA and developed the most widely used system for evaluating and selecting puppies. Her film *Puppy Aptitude Testing* was named Best Film on

Dogs for 1980 by the DWAA. She also devised a Personality Profile for dogs to help owners gain a better understanding of why their pets do what they do. Her article "Drives—A New Look at an Old Concept" was named Best Article in a Specialty Magazine for 1991 by the DWAA.

She specializes in behavior, nutrition and alternative sources of health care such as acupuncture and homeopathy, and she has formulated a balanced, homemade diet for dogs. Wendy is a member of the Animal Behavior Society and the Advisory Board of the North American Wildlife Foundation, and has lectured at the prestigious Natural History Museum in London.

The Volhards continue to be active trainers and exhibitors who have obtained over forty Obedience titles, multiple High in Trial awards and Dog World Awards of Canine Distinction with their Landseer Newfoundlands, Yorkshire Terrier, Standard Wirehaired Dachshund, Labrador Retriever and German Shepherd Dog.

Acknowledgments

WE GRATEFULLY ACKNOWLEDGE Jim Dearinger, vice president of Obedience of the American Kennel Club, for his availability, support, encouragement and sound advice; Robert McKowen, AKC vice president of Performance Events; and Jackie Fraser, manager Canine Good Citizen and Special Projects of the American Kennel Club, for keeping us up-to-date on the latest revisions.

Art Clogg, of Fredericton, New Brunswick, Canada, contributed much time and effort in the refinement of our Canine Personality Profile, for which we thank him.

We also want to thank the following instructors for the time they devoted to conducting the Canine Good Citizen Test at our five-day training camps: Sue Bickel, Judy Fox, Marcia Kmetz Majors and Mary Ann Zeigenfuse.

The compilation of the "Pack Leader's Bill of Rights" and "How to Become a Pack Leader" was done by the instructors of Cranbourne Dog Training School of London, England—Sheila Hamilton Andrews, Ian Wright, Gail Ward and Kt Rourke—and we thank them for permitting us to include these in this book.

Finally, we are again indebted to Melissa Bartlett for her wonderful drawings. She is the co-author of *What All Good Dogs Should Know: The Sensible Way to Train*, and has illustrated various other projects for us, including four books. Her insights into dog behavior, combined with her talent and sense of humor, make her illustrations particularly meaningful and telling.

Foreword

I MET JACK AND WENDY VOLHARD shortly after 1973, the year I became director of Obedience of the American Kennel Club (AKC) and we have become good friends since then. At that time they had the most beautiful and spirited Landseer Newfoundlands I had ever seen, which they trained and exhibited with enormous success.

The Volhards developed an approach to training, which they call the Motivational Method. It is designed to do just that—motivate the owner *and* the dog. The Motivational Method is grounded on a thorough knowledge of how people learn and of dog behavior. Since 1983 they have authored or co-authored four major books on dog training and teaching dog Obedience classes, and have produced four video tapes.

Over the years I would frequently consult with Jack on a variety of issues confronting the AKC. I came to appreciate his analytical approach as well as his keen insight, which no doubt was sharpened by being an active exhibitor as well as an AKC Obedience judge.

Wendy has few equals when it comes to understanding canine behavior. She has a remarkable ability to sense the needs of a particular dog and do what is best for the animal. A talent, for sure, but one she has honed to a fine point by studious research into all phases of the dog—behavior, health, nutrition, structure and training.

I had the pleasure of being the guest speaker at two of their five-day training camps, which are held three times a year. I am extremely pleased that they have added the Canine Good Citizen test to these camps and that it has been a big hit there. I am equally pleased that they have written this book on the Canine Good Citizen. I cannot think of anyone else who could have done a better job. This book contains everything the reader needs to know about training any dog to become a Canine Good Citizen. Still, there is much more—the book shares a wealth of insights for the beginner, as well as the experienced dog person.

The book's best feature is that it gives each person the means to tailor the training to the individual dog's character and temperament. It thoroughly explains what makes dogs different and how these differences dictate the approach to training that needs to be taken.

I highly recommend this book to those who want to know more about their dogs and who are interested in training for the Canine Good Citizen.

James E. Dearinger
AKC Vice President, Obedience
New York, N.Y.

Introduction

The American Kennel Club's Canine Good Citizen program was developed to promote responsible dog ownership in a manner that would be easy for both dog and owner. Any book that promotes and encourages dog owners to participate is doing a public service, and this book does it well.

By providing certification to both pure-bred dogs and mixed breeds, the CGC encompasses all of the dogs affected by canine legislation. Through encouraging people to provide enough training to make their dogs useful citizens, the CGC program helps eliminate restrictive dog legislation designed by well-meaning if sometimes poorly informed lawmakers.

This book is aptly named. Yes, every dog can be a good citizen if their owners care enough to make it happen. The key is to encourage dog owners everywhere to be responsible enough to make their dogs a pleasure to be around and able to handle most situations that they might be expected to encounter in everyday life.

It is easy to become involved in the CGC program. Tests are offered throughout the United States for those who wish to certify their dogs. This book not only encourages participating but provides useful information on how to do it.

Robert H. McKowen
Vice President
Performance Events
American Kennel Club

THE CANINE GOOD CITIZEN
Every Dog Can Be One

A trained dog is a member of the family.

1

Why a Canine Good Citizen?

AS A GIFT to yourself, your dog and your neighbors, train your dog to become a Canine Good Citizen. It will mean sanity for you, safety for your dog and compliments from your neighbors.

Canine Good Citizens are close to being perfect pets. They are welcome almost anywhere because they behave themselves around people and other dogs. They are a pleasure to take for a walk and can be taken on trips and family outings. They are members of the family in every sense of the word.

Untrained dogs have few, if any, privileges. When guests come, unruly dogs are locked in the basement because they are too unruly. When the family sits down to eat, dogs are put outside because they beg at the table. Nobody wants to take them for a walk because they pull, and these dogs never get to go on family outings because they are such a nuisance.

Dogs have a life expectancy of eight to sixteen years. Now is the time to ensure these years are going to be mutually rewarding. Teach your dog to be that perfect pet you always wanted—a Canine Good Citizen.

WHAT IS INVOLVED IN TRAINING MAX?

This book describes an eight-week training program to turn Max from an exuberant lout into a Canine Good Citizen in just a few minutes a day. It will take considerably fewer than eight weeks, if Max is a willing pupil. Much of what you will teach can be and should be combined with your regular routine of feeding, walking and grooming Max. After you have gone through the program and passed the Canine Good Citizen test, frequent reviews of the lessons will keep Max on the straight and narrow. Think of Max's lessons as you would of memorizing a poem—if it is not periodically recited, it will be forgotten.

BUILDING TRUST

Picture Max chasing a cat across the road. Your heart is in your mouth because you are afraid he might get run over. When Max finally returns, you are angry and soundly scold him for chasing the cat and giving you such a scare.

But . . . here is how *your dog* looks at this situation. First, he chased the cat, which was lots of fun. Then he came back to you and was reprimanded, which was no fun at all.

What you *wanted* to teach your dog was not to chase the cat. What you *actually* taught was that coming to you can be unpleasant.

Lesson: Whether you are pleased or angry, your dog associates these feelings only with what he did *last*.

One of the commands you will want your dog to learn is to come when called. To be successful, remember this principle: *Whenever your dog comes to you, be nice.* Reward the dog for coming to you.

No matter what, be pleasant and greet your dog with a kind word, a pat on the head and a smile. Teach your dog to trust you by *being* a safe place for him. When he is with you, follows you or comes to you, make your dog feel wanted. When you call Max to you and then punish him, you undermine his trust in you. When Max comes to you on his own and you punish him, he thinks he is being punished for coming to you.

You may ask, "How can I be nice to my dog when he brings

Whenever your dog comes to you, be nice.

me the remains of one of my brand new shoes, or when he wants to jump on me with muddy paws, or when I just discovered an unwanted present on the carpet?''

The answers are not rooted in discipline, but are found in training, prevention and understanding your dog.

CONSISTENCY

If there is any magic to training, it is *consistency*. Your dog cannot understand the concepts of sometimes, maybe, perhaps or only on Sundays. Your dog *can* and does understand yes and no.

For example, it is confusing when you encourage jumping up on you when you are wearing old clothes, but then become angry when your dog joyfully plants muddy paws on your best suit.

Does this mean you can never permit your puppy to jump up on you? Not at all, but you have to train your pup that this is permitted *only* when you say it's OK. But beware: It is more difficult to train a dog to make this distinction than to train one not to jump up at all. The more "black and white" or "yes and no" you can make it, the easier it will be for your dog to understand what you want and the more pleased you will be with the results.

Similarly, learn to become consistent in your communications with your dog. If you sharply clap your hands together with a loud "Stop it" every time you want Max to stop whatever he is doing, you probably will not get a response to clapping as an enticement to come to you.

Lastly, be sure every member of the family handles the dog the same way and uses the same commands, including the children. If you don't want your dog to beg at the table, *nobody* should slip treats under the table.

PERSISTENCE AND PATIENCE

Training your dog is a question of who is more persistent—you or your dog. Some things will be learned quickly; others will take more time. If several tries don't bring success, be patient, remain calm and try again. It sometimes takes many repetitions before a dog understands a command and responds to it each and every time. Remember, too, that the dog does not speak English, so raising your voice does not help either. Quite the contrary, it may be frightening and even prevent the dog from learning.

ELIMINATING "NO" FROM YOUR DOG VOCABULARY

Before you get started with the actual training of your dog, we want you to focus on the way in which you communicate with Max. Does Max perceive the interaction as positive or negative, pleasant or unpleasant, friendly or unfriendly. For example, how many times do you use the word "No," and how many times do you say "Good dog" when communicating with your dog? It has been our experience during the more than twenty-five years of teaching dog training classes that by the time we see the dogs, most have been "No'ed" to death. Everything the dog does brings forth a stern "Don't do this," "Don't do that," "No, bad dog." The dogs are

Eliminate "No" from your training vocabulary . . .

. . . and substitute a **positive** command for a negative one.

sick of it and have no interest or desire in learning what the owners want them to do. It is for this reason we recommend that you eliminate the word "No" from your dog training vocabulary.

Whenever possible you should substitute a positive for a negative. For example, when your dog jumps on you, instead of yelling "No, Max, Down, Max, get off or I'll kill you," teach him to sit on command. Now when he jumps, or even better, when he is thinking of jumping on you, say "Sit." When you get the right response, sincerely praise him with "What a good dog you are."

In your dealings with your dog, ask yourself, "What exactly do I want Max to do or not to do?" Use a "Do" command instead of a reprimand wherever possible so you can praise your dog. You will find *there is a direct relationship between your dog's willingness to cooperate and your attitude.* Get out of the "blaming" habit of assuming it's the dog's fault. Your dog only does what comes naturally. Your job is to show Max what you expect in a positive way.

There are going to be times when you will have to use a verbal reprimand, for which we suggest "Stop it." We reserve it for situations where we can't think of a positive command or where the dog has not been sufficiently trained so that one would work. During the training process you should not need to use the command at all.

Another unsatisfactory way of communicating with your dog is to use only the dog's name, but changing your tone of voice— pleading, cajoling, promising, threatening, begging—to whatever the circumstances demand. Some of us are not even aware we are doing it. Either way, it's a bad habit that should be stopped.

STAYING ONE STEP AHEAD

After living with your dog for some time, you can pretty much tell what's on his mind just by observing him. A dog's facial expressions and body movements are quite expressive and forecast Max's intentions, if you pay close attention. The direction and movement of the whiskers, eyes and ears are all indications that the little wheels are turning. Your prior experience tells you what Max is thinking. For example, you can tell when Max is about to chase after a cat, a jogger or a bicycle. It is at that point that you interrupt this thought process by giving a command, such as "Sit" or "Come," or as a last resort "Stop it."

6

Your dog will tell you what's on his/her mind and you can interrupt that thought process.

What if you weren't paying attention and Max is off on a mad dash after the neighbor's cat? You may be able to stop Max in mid-stride and have him return to you with a firm "Max, Come." If not, and he chases the cat clear out of the yard, then what? Should you reprimand Max as he returns to you? Obviously not, and the best course of action is to ignore the incident and make a mental note to be more alert to such eventualities.

What about the situation where you return home from a hard day at work and you discover that Max has chewed your favorite slippers to a frazzle? You are furious and call Max, confront him with the ruined slippers, yelling at the top of your lungs, "How could you do this to me? After all I have done for you? Have you no shame?" Worse yet, you may hit the poor dog.

The problem with this approach is that your dog doesn't have the slightest idea *why* you are upset. Max, no doubt, will look

Don't undermine your relationship with your dog with after-the-fact discipline.

dutifully guilty, knowing you are *upset*, and he may even grasp that you are upset at *him*, but he does *not know* it is because of the slippers he chewed. That is a connection he can't make. If you attribute human qualities and reasoning abilities to your dog, your efforts at training are doomed to frustration and failure.

Your pet certainly does not experience guilt. The old "go to your room without supper" routine does not work any better with dogs than it does with children. Blaming your dog because he or she "ought to know better" is absurd. If dogs knew better, they wouldn't have done it in the first place. Max did enjoy chewing the slippers and no matter what you do now, you can't make him unenjoy it.

As a practical matter, all you can do is ignore it and learn from the experience to keep your slippers in a safe place. "After the deed'' discipline is not only ineffective, but undermines the relationship you are trying to build and causes your dog's distrust of you.

The order of effectiveness for dealing with unwanted behavior is:

1. Interrupting the thought process, that is, when your dog is *thinking* about the unwanted behavior and before he has had a chance to set it in motion.
2. Catching your dog in the act and preventing him from completing the unwanted behavior is the next best choice.

After your dog has executed the unwanted behavior, *ignore it*. The further removed from the event in point of time, the less effective remedial efforts will be.

TAKING CHARGE

It's not a matter of choice. Since dogs are pack animals, you and your family are now the pack. As far as your dogs are concerned, no pack can exist without a leader, and it's either you or them. That's the way it *has* to be.

You may think that you really just want to be friends, partners or peers with your dog. You can be all of those, but for the well-being of your dog you must be the one in charge. In today's complicated world you cannot rely on your pet to make the decisions.

Few dogs actively seek leadership and most are perfectly con-

For your dog's safety, *you* have to be in charge.

Without leadership, even the meekest dog will take over.

tent for you to assume that role, as long as you do. But you *must* do so, or even the meekest of dogs will try to take over. Remember, it's not a matter of choice. For everyone's safety, you have to be the one in charge.

PACK LEADER'S BILL OF RIGHTS

Cranbourne Dog Training School of London, England, which teaches our approach to training, has compiled the following "Pack Leader's Bill of Rights" for its students and has given us permission to share it with you.

10

How to become pack leader.

Pack Leader's Bill of Rights

1. To eat first, gorge themselves and own any pickings left over.
2. To stand, sit or lie down wherever they want.
3. To have access to the "prime" spots in the household.
4. To control entry to or from any room in the house.
5. To proceed through all narrow openings first.
6. To initiate the hunt and dictate where to hunt.
7. To make the "kill" at the end of the hunt.
8. To demand attention from subordinate pack members.
9. To ignore or actively discourage unwanted attention.
10. To restrict the movements of lesser-ranking pack members.
11. To win all games.

By studying this Bill of Rights you can tell who is the pack leader in your house. If you think it is your dog, you can become pack leader by adhering to the following dos and don'ts, also compiled by Cranbourne Dog Training School.

11

How to Become a Pack Leader

Do	Don't
Eat before you feed your dog.	*Feed your dog first.*
Restrict access to your bedrooms and furniture.	*Let your dog sleep in or on your bed.*
Take the shortest route to your destination and make your dog move out of your way.	*Let your dog restrict your access to anything in the house or take up residence in a doorway.*
Proceed first through narrow passages.	*Let your dog bound out ahead of you.*
Run in the *opposite* direction if your dog "takes off" on a walk.	*Chase your dog yelling "Come!"*
Take your dog's "kills" (stolen articles or food) away.	*Allow your dog to keep or play with the "kill."*
Call your dog *to you* to give affection.	*Go over to your dog to give affection.*
Ignore or discourage pawing, nudging, whining.	*Give attention when your dog demands it.*
Ignore your dog first thing in the morning, when you get home or when you come in.	*Make a large fuss over your dog whenever he demands that you do so.*
Restrict the dog's movements with the "Long Down" exercise.	*Give more than one command or give up.*
Initiate games with your dog, make sure you win them and end up with possession of the toy.	*Play games, especially tug of war, if you can't win, or give the toy to your dog after the game is over.*
Reward your dog for completing an exercise well.	*Give more than one command, or **any** command if you are not prepared to reinforce it.*

The more *don'ts* that are allowed, the more likely Max is to become pack leader and the less successful your efforts at training will be. The more *dos* you consistently enforce, the greater is Max's respect for you and the more successful you will be in your efforts to train him.

SIGNS TO WATCH FOR

Does your dog take over your favorite armchair? Is he constantly demanding attention? Does he ignore you when you want him to move, or shoot out of doors ahead of you? If so, he is in charge and not you.

Part of his behavior may be caused by lack of education and the first order of business is for you to begin *training him*. Begin with the next section, "Getting Started," and then teach your dog Sit and Lie Down on command as described in Chapter 6. Both of these exercises not only help you to control your dog, but they also teach the dog to accept that you are in charge.

After you have trained your dog, retain your leadership by using on a regular basis the exercises you have taught Max. For example:

1. Make your dog Sit before giving meals, or *any* treat.
2. Make your dog Sit before being petted.
3. Make your dog Sit and Stay before going through a door.

Begin the leadership training as soon as possible after you have obtained your dog. Then use **leadership exercises** consistently to make it clear to your dog that you are in charge. You will then have a dog who looks to you for leadership and one that is a real joy to have around.

GETTING STARTED

Before you do anything else, you first want to settle who is in charge of your "pack." We prefer to address that issue with leadership exercises so that the actual training can truly be as much fun as it is supposed to be. For this purpose we have devised a simple four-week leadership program.

The program consists of the thirty-minute Down and the ten-minute Sit, each done three times a week, on alternate days. Both can be practiced while you are watching TV or reading, so long as you keep an eye on Max. Concurrently, you can start on teaching the specific exercises you want Max to learn for the Canine Good Citizen test.

> **Note:** You may find that you do not have the time or opportunity to get a Canine Good Citizen Certificate (title) or train your dog toward that goal or even get beyond this chapter. Whatever your circumstances may be and without doing anything else, you will have a better pet and companion if you use and follow the four sequences of our leadership program.

Week One

- Sit Max at your left side. Kneel next to him, both of you facing in the same direction.
- Drape your left arm across the dog's shoulder and hold your hand, palm up, behind his left foreleg just below the elbow.
- Place your right hand behind the right foreleg.
- Supporting your dog's forelegs on your palms, lift Max into the begging position and lower him onto the ground with a Down command.
- When you lift Max into the begging position, keep your thumbs either up or folded in your palms so that you cannot accidentally apply pressure on the forelegs.
- Should you forget and squeeze the legs with your thumbs, your dog will try and pull his legs away and you may wind up in a wrestling match.
- Take your hands off Max and keep still.
- Every time your dog gets up, put him back.
- After thirty minutes give the release word "OK," even if he has fallen asleep.
- Practice this exercise three times during the training week on alternate days.

Most dogs, after several attempts at getting up, resign themselves to remaining in position for the thirty minutes. Some, on the

Placing your dog in the "Down" position.

other hand, literally kick and scream almost the entire time. It is the latter who need this exercise the most and you will have to remain patient and calm. You will also want to increase the frequency of this exercise to every day. If your dog is really bouncy, you may want to teach this exercise on a leash. Sit in a chair next to the dog and then sit on the leash so your hands are free to put Max into position.

At all times remember the purpose of this exercise is to teach your dog (in a calm and nonviolent manner) who is in charge and for your dog to accept you as pack leader. Your ability to physically place and keep your dog in the Down position is an absolutely necessary component of that purpose. *We cannot overstate the value of this exercise.*

Once your dog accepts you as leader, all further training will go smoothly. As long as there is a question about who is the boss, at some point in your training, Max, in effect, will say ''Today I don't do this.'' Obviously, that makes your dog unreliable, not a desirable result.

Week Two

This week, sit in a chair next to Max as you practice the thirty-minute Down. For the ten-minute Sit, place Max into a Sit as follows:

- With Max standing at your left side, both of you facing in the same direction, place your right hand against his chest and your left hand on his shoulders.
- With your left hand stroke down the entire length of the dog's back, over the tail all the way to the dog's knees.
- With equal pressure of the right hand and the left, fold Max into a Sit with the command ''Sit.''
- Take your hands off the dog and keep still.
- Every time Max moves, put him back.
- After ten minutes, use the release word ''OK.''

Practice the thirty-minute Down and the ten-minute Sit three times each on alternate days during the training week.

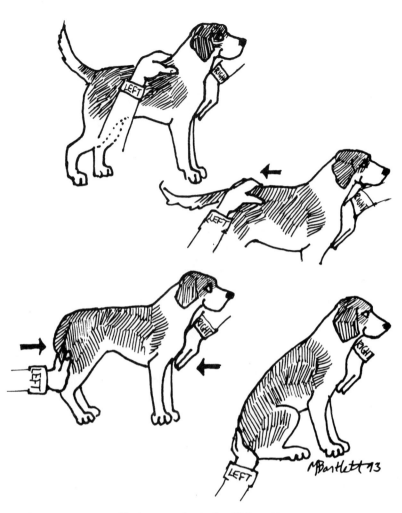

Placing your dog in the "Sit" position.

Week Three

When you practice the thirty-minute Down and the ten-minute Sit with Max this week, sit across the room from him. Make sure you put him back if he should move.

Week Four

This week, move about the room while Max remains in position, but do not leave the room.

After you have successfully completed this four-week program, your dog will understand that *you are in charge.* Even so, as the dog matures, there may be times when Max will buck for a promotion and you will have to review the thirty-minute Down once or twice a week—just as a reminder that you are still the one in charge.

SUMMARY

1) A trained dog is a loved dog.
2) You need persistence and patience to train a dog.
3) Whenever your dog comes to you, be nice.
4) If there is any magic to training, it is consistency.
5) As far as your dog is concerned, no pack can exist without a leader, and it's either you or him.
6) For safety, *you* have to be the one in charge.

2

What Is a Canine Good Citizen?

A CANINE GOOD CITIZEN is a dog that is well behaved around people as well as other dogs, at home and in public. It is the kind of dog that you want to own, one that is safe with children and one that you would welcome as a neighbor. It is a dog that is a pleasure to own and a nuisance to no one. To become a Canine Good Citizen your dog must demonstrate, by means of a short test, that he or she meets these requirements.

Author of the Canine Good Citizen (CGC) is James E. Dearinger, vice president of Obedience of the American Kennel Club. Although other individuals had advanced similar proposals over the years, it was Dearinger who devised the original test and, perhaps more importantly, who persuaded the American Kennel Club to adopt it. It is unique in a number of ways, not the least of which is that *it is the only AKC sponsored activity that includes mixed breeds*. The concept of a Canine Good Citizen is based on the premise that **all** dogs should be trained.

After approximately two years of experience with the Canine Good Citizen test, the AKC Performance Events Division contacted

Olympic USA Gold Medal winner, Peter Vidmar, and his Golden Retriever, Thunder, receiving the CGC from James Dearinger. *Photo by Hal Randall*

more than 4,000 training organizations eliciting comments and suggestions about the program. The input received was reviewed by an advisory committee and resulted in a number of refinements and revisions authored by Jacqueline Fraser, Manager CGC and Special Projects, Performances Events Division, and her assistant, Lori Pepe.

L. L. Bean, CGC, the authors' Lab.   *Photo by Jack Volhard*

The Canine Good Citizen is an examination using a series of exercises or tests that evaluate the dog's ability to behave in an acceptable manner in public. Its purpose is to demonstrate that the dog, as a companion for all people, can be a respected member of the community and can be trained and conditioned to always behave in the home, in public places and in the presence of other dogs in a

21

manner that will reflect credit on the dog. The examination consists of the following ten tests, all of which are scored on a pass/fail system:

1. **ACCEPTING A FRIENDLY STRANGER**

   Demonstrates that the dog will allow a friendly stranger to approach and speak to the handler in a natural, everyday situation.

   The evaluator walks up to the dog and handler, and greets the handler in a friendly manner, ignoring the dog.

   The evaluator and handler shake hands and exchange pleasantries. The dog must show no sign of resentment or shyness and *must not break position* or try to go to the evaluator.

2. **SITTING POLITELY FOR PETTING**

   Demonstrates that the dog will allow a friendly stranger to touch it while it is out with the owner/handler. With the dog sitting at the handler's side (either side is permissible) throughout the exercise, the evaluator pets the dog on the head and body *only*. The handler may talk to his or her dog throughout the exercise.

   After petting, the evaluator then circles the dog and handler, completing the test. The dog must not show shyness or resentment.

3. **APPEARANCE AND GROOMING**

   Demonstrates that the dog will welcome being groomed and examined and will permit a stranger, such as a veterinarian, groomer or friend of the owner, to do so. It also demonstrates the owner's care, concern and responsibility.

   The evaluator inspects the dog to determine if it is clean and groomed. The dog must appear to be in a healthy condition (i.e., proper weight, clean, healthy and alert). The handler should supply the comb or brush commonly used on the dog.

The concept of a Canine Good Citizen.

The evaluator then easily combs or brushes the dog, and in a natural manner, lightly examines the ears and gently picks up each front foot.

It is not necessary for the dog to hold a specific position during the examination, and the handler may talk to the dog, praise and give encouragement throughout.

23

Appearance and grooming. Participants in the Canine Good Citizen test at the Volhards' April 1994 Training Camp. (See also pages 27–29.)

4. OUT FOR A WALK (WALKING ON A LOOSE LEASH)

Demonstrates that the handler is in control of the dog. The dog may be on either side of the handler, whichever the handler prefers.

(**Note:** The left-side position is required in AKC obedience competition and all activities where the dog is in service to the handler, such as guiding the blind.)

The dog's position should leave no doubt that the dog is attentive to the handler and is responding to the handler's movements and changes of direction. The dog need not be perfectly aligned with the handler and need not sit when the handler stops.

The evaluator may use a pre-plotted course or may direct the handler/dog team by issuing instructions or commands. In either case, there must be a Left Turn, Right Turn and About Turn, with at least one Stop in between and another at the end. The handler may talk to the dog along the way to praise or command in a normal tone of voice. The handler may also Sit the dog at the Halt, if desired.

Walking on a loose leash.

5. WALKING THROUGH A CROWD

Demonstrates that the dog can move about politely in pedestrian traffic and is under control in public places.

The dog and handler walk around and pass close to several people (at least three). The dog may show some interest in the strangers but should continue to walk with the handler, without evidence of overexuberance, shyness or resentment. The handler may talk to the dog and encourage or praise the dog throughout the test. The dog should not be straining at the leash.

(**Note:** Children may act as members of the crowd in this test, as well as in Test 9. However, whenever children participate in a test they must be instructed on their role and be supervised. It is permissible to have one dog in a crowd but the dog must be on lead and well mannered.)

6. SIT AND DOWN ON COMMAND STAYING IN PLACE

Demonstrates that the dog has training, will respond to the handler's commands to Sit and Down and will remain in the place commanded by the handler (Sit or Down position, whichever the handler prefers).

Prior to this test, the dog's leash is replaced with a 20-foot line. The handler may take a reasonable amount of time and use more than one command to make the dog Sit and then Down. The evaluator must determine if the dog has responded to the handler's commands. The handler may not force the dog into either position but may touch the dog to offer gentle guidance.

When instructed by the evaluator, the handler tells the dog "Stay" and, with the 20-foot line in hand, walks forward the length of the line, turns and returns to the dog at a natural pace (the 20-foot line is not removed or dropped). The dog must remain in the place in which he or she was left (the dog may change position) until the evaluator instructs the handler to release the dog. The dog may be released from the front or the side.

7. PRAISE/INTERACTION

(**Note:** As a practical matter the Praise/Interaction test should follow the release of the dog from Test 6.)

Demonstrates that the dog can be easily calmed following play or praise and can leave the area of this test in a mannerly fashion.

This test should not be more than ten seconds in duration and begins when, on the evaluator's instruction, the dog is released from Test 6.

26

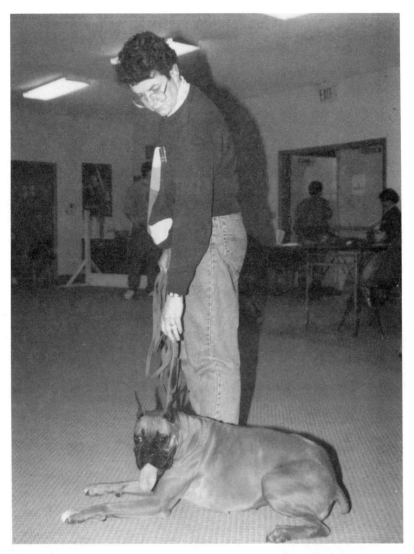

Staying in place.   *Photo by Suzi Swygert*

The handler may use one or any combination of verbal praise, petting, playing with a toy (tossed or handed to the dog) or performing a favorite trick—but not food. The dog may actively play or simply be passively agreeable to praise. When the evaluator calls time, the handler will calm the dog for the next test. The handler's voice may

27

be firm but should not be loud or angry. Slight leash pressure is acceptable.

8. REACTION TO ANOTHER DOG

Demonstrates that the dog can behave politely around other dogs.

Two handlers and their dogs approach each other from a distance of about 10 yards, stop, shake hands and exchange pleasantries, and continue on for about 5 yards.

Reaction to another dog.　　　　　　　　*Photo by Suzi Swygert*

28

The dogs should show no more than casual interest in each other. Neither dog should go to the other dog or its handler.

9. REACTION TO DISTRACTIONS

Demonstrates that the dog is confident at all times when faced with common distracting situations.

The evaluator will select *only two* from the following list:

(**Note:** Since some dogs are sensitive to sound and others to visual distractions, choose one sound and one visual distraction.)

a) A person using crutches, a wheelchair or a walker. This distraction simulates a disabled person who requires the use of service equipment.
b) A sudden closing or opening of a door.
c) Dropping a large book, no closer than 10 feet behind the dog.

Reaction to distractions.   *Photo by Suzi Swygert*

d) A jogger running in front of the dog.

e) Good-natured pushing and shoving or animated, excited talk and back-slapping by persons, with the dog and handler passing within 10 feet.

f) A person pushing a cart approaching from the front or rear, passing within 10 feet.

g) A person on a bicycle approaching from the front or rear, passing about 6 feet to the side of the dog.

h) Knocking over a chair, no closer that 6 feet from the dog.

The dog may express a natural interest and curiosity and may appear slightly startled but should not panic, try to run away, show aggressiveness or bark. The handler may talk to the dog and use encouragement or praise throughout the exercise.

10. SUPERVISED ISOLATION

Demonstrates that the dog can be left alone if necessary, and will maintain skills learned in training and good manners.

The handler will fasten the dog to a 6-foot line and go to a place out of sight of the dog for three minutes. The dog *should not* continually bark, whine, howl, pace unnecessarily or show anything other than *mild* agitation or nervousness. This is *not* a Stay exercise; dogs may stand, sit, lie down *and* change positions during this test.

Dogs are tested individually, not as a group. More than one dog can be tested at a time, provided there is no visual contact between these dogs.

(**Note:** This test is designed to determine if the dog can be left alone without causing a stressful situation, but *AKC does not endorse tying out as a general practice*. Evaluators are encouraged to say something like, "Would you like me to watch your dog while you make your call?" This adds a touch of reality and accentuates the fact that leaving a dog tied and unsupervised is *not* condoned. Evaluators should watch the dog from an unobtrusive position.)

These are practical tests that determine the amount of control you have over your dog and the dog's ability to behave appropriately in public. The evaluators, in addition to deciding the dog's ability to pass these exercises, are asked to consider if this is:

1. The kind of dog he or she would like to own.
2. The kind of dog that would be safe with children.
3. The kind of dog he or she would welcome as a neighbor.
4. The kind of dog that makes the owner happy and isn't making someone else unhappy.

It would be nice if dogs came that way, but almost all require at least some training to become a Canine Good Citizen. Some of this training is formal and some of it no more than the manners that every dog needs to know to be an enjoyable pet, and the type of training every responsible dog owner would undertake on his or her own. Responsible dog owners recognize that their dog's behavior is a reflection of their commitment to create a positive image of their dogs and dogs in general. Hence, the Canine Good Citizen is an ideal forum to demonstrate that commitment and to lead by example.

Since its inception on September 1, 1989, the Canine Good Citizen has become the fastest growing and most popular program in AKC history, and it has become a regular feature at our five-day training camps. Moreover, other organizations such as the Delta Society and Therapy Dogs International have adopted parts or all of the Canine Good Citizen into their respective programs. Several states, Florida being the first, have passed resolutions endorsing the Canine Good Citizen program as a means of teaching responsible pet ownership, and as a means of teaching dogs Canine Good Citizen behaviors for the community.

Today, the Canine Good Citizen program is offered by many training organizations and the test itself has become a popular adjunct at dog shows. Dog organizations in other countries, notably England and Japan, are becoming interested in using the Canine Good Citizen test.

Join the ranks of those who have obtained their Canine Good Citizen certificates and titles. Ideally, every dog should be trained to become a Canine Good Citizen, and the more that are, the better the chances of counteracting the growing anti-dog sentiments in many communities. Irresponsible dog ownership has been the cause for this sentiment and only responsible pet ownership can reverse it. Demonstrate that your dog is an effective personal companion and a member in good standing with the community by training him to become a Canine Good Citizen.

SUMMARY

1) A Canine Good Citizen is a dog that is well behaved around people and other dogs, at home and in public.
2) The Canine Good Citizen examination tests the dog's ability to behave in an acceptable manner in public.
3) The Canine Good Citizen examination consists of ten practical tests that determine the amount of control you have over your dog.
4) Responsible dog owners recognize that their dog's behavior is a reflection of their commitment to create a positive image of dogs.
5) The Canine Good Citizen has become a fast growing and popular AKC program.
6) The Canine Good Citizen is the best way to counteract anti-dog sentiment.

3

What Happens When?

$\mathbf{F}$ROM BIRTH THROUGH MATURITY, your dog experiences various physical and mental developmental periods. These, in turn, affect the dog's behavior.

THE FORTY-NINTH DAY AND BONDING

Weeks Seven Through Twelve

The age at which a puppy is separated from its mother and littermates influences behaviors important to becoming a good pet. At about the forty-ninth day of life, when the puppy is neurologically complete, that special attachment between dogs and their owners, called "*bonding*," starts. For this reason, this is the ideal time for puppies to leave the nest for their new homes.

A puppy separated from its canine family before that day, say at the thirty-fifth day (fifth week), may develop an unhealthy attachment to humans. Typical behaviors are the dog's overprotectiveness of the owner and aggression toward other dogs, nervousness and excessive barking.

From the thirty-fifth day on, the mother also teaches her pup-

Too EARLY— OVERLY ATTACHED TO HUMANS

7 to 12 weeks— BEST TIME FOR BONDING TO OWNER

TOO LATE — LITTLE ATTACHMENT TO HUMANS

Puppy/human bonding continuum.

pies basic doggie manners. She communicates to the puppies what is unacceptable behavior and, if necessary, growls, snarls or snaps at them as a form of discipline. For example, during the weaning process she teaches the puppies to leave her alone. After just a few repetitions, the puppies begin to respond to a mere look or a curled lip from mother. A puppy that has not had these important lessons may have difficulty in accepting discipline while growing up.

A puppy left with the mother or littermates for much longer than the twelfth week will grow up being too dog-oriented. With each passing day, the pup loses a little of the ability to adapt to a new environment. Bonding to humans will be difficult, if possible at all, as will be teaching the dog to accept responsibility for its own behavior. The dog will not care about its human family and will be more difficult to train, including housetraining.

THE NEED TO SOCIALIZE

Weeks Seven Through Twelve

Your dog is a social animal. To become an acceptable pet, the pup needs to interact with you and your family, as well as other humans and dogs during the seventh through the twelfth week of life. If denied that, your dog's behavior around other people or dogs may be unpredictable—either fearful or perhaps even aggressive. For example, unless regularly exposed to children during this period, a dog may not be comfortable or trustworthy around them.

Your puppy needs the chance to meet and to have positive experiences with those beings that will play a role in his or her life.

34

The mother dog disciplines the puppy.

If you are a grandparent whose grandchildren occasionally visit, have your puppy meet children as often as you can. If you live by yourself, but have friends visit you, make an effort to let your puppy meet other people, particularly members of the opposite sex. If you plan on taking your puppy to an Obedience class or dog shows or ultimately using the dog in a breeding program, you should both be interacting with other dogs.

If you plan to take your dog on family outings or vacations, introduce riding in a car. Time spent *now* is well worth the effort. It will result in a well-adjusted adult companion dog.

Socialize your puppy.

This is also a time when your puppy will follow your every footstep. Encourage this behavior by rewarding the puppy with an occasional treat, a pat on the head or a kind word.

FEAR PERIOD

Weeks Eight Through Twelve

Avoid exposing the puppy to traumatic experiences during this period because they may have a lasting impact. For example, elective surgery, such as ear cropping, should be done, *if at all*, before eight or after eleven weeks of age. When you have to take your puppy to the veterinarian have the doctor give the puppy a treat before, during and after the examination to make the visit a pleasant experience. A particularly stressful or unpleasant experience now can literally ruin a puppy for life.

During the first year's growth you may see fear reactions at other times. When you do, under no circumstances drag your puppy up to the object that caused the fear. On the other hand don't pet or reassure the dog—you may create the impression that you approve of this behavior. Rather, distract the puppy and go on to something that is pleasant. After a short time, the fearful behavior will disappear.

36

BOOGA
BOOGA

Avoid exposing your puppy to traumatic experiences during the fear period.

LEAVING HOME

Four to Eight Months

Sometime between the fourth and eighth months, your puppy will begin to realize there is a big, wide world out there. Up to now, every time you have called, the pup willingly came to you. But now, your dog may want to wander off and investigate. The dog is maturing and cutting the apron strings. This is normal. Your puppy is not being spiteful or disobedient, just becoming an adolescent.

While going through this phase, it is best to keep the pup on leash or in a confined area until your pet has learned to come when called. Otherwise, not coming when called will become a habit annoying to you and dangerous to the dog. Once this becomes a pattern, it will be difficult to change, and prevention is the best cure. It is much easier to teach your dog to come when called *before* developing the habit of running away. Chapter 9 teaches you how to train your dog to come when called.

Under *no* circumstances play the game of chasing the dog.

Never run after your puppy—instead, run the other way and have your puppy chase you.

Instead, run the *other* way and try to get your *dog* to *chase you*. If that does not work, kneel on the ground and pretend you have found something extremely interesting, hoping your puppy's curiosity will bring the dog to you. If you do have to go to the dog, approach slowly until you can calmly take hold of the collar.

During this time your puppy also goes through teething and needs to chew—anything and everything. Dogs, like children, can't help it. Your job is to provide acceptable outlets for this need, such as chew bones and toys. If one of your favorite shoes is demolished try to control yourself. Puppies have the irritating habit of tackling many shoes, but only *one* from each pair. Look at it as a lesson to keep your possessions out of reach. Scolding will not stop the need to chew, but it may cause your pet to fear you.

GROWING UP

One to Four Years

No matter how much we might wish that cute little puppy to remain as is, your pup is going to grow up.

Maturity rates vary from breed to breed. Generally, the larger the dog, the longer it takes to become an adult. It happens anywhere from one to four years. During that time, a dog will undergo physical and emotional changes. For you, as the owner, the most important one is the dog's sense of identity. To put it in a nutshell, every so

38

Confinement

Suitable toys

Exercise

Developing good behavior.

often your dog may push for a promotion, trying to be the one in charge, telling *you* what to do *instead* of the other way around. Again, this is perfectly normal and all it requires is training the dog to understand who is in charge.

PREDICTABLE PROBLEMS—POSSIBLE CAUSES AND SOLUTIONS

During the time you have Daisy, you will experience difficulties that are predictable. Some of these you can avoid or forestall, and others you can't. For example, an illness such as an infection may cause accidents in the house, or anxiety, lethargy and some-

Training your dog to understand who is in charge.

times aggression. If you notice a change in Daisy's behavior, take her to the veterinarian for a checkup.

Excessive barking, chewing and **digging**, and **self-mutilation** are **problems** often associated with boredom, isolation and mental stagnation. Dogs are pack animals that need regular interaction with the "pack" members, that is, you and your family. Just spending time together may be enough, but challenging the dog's mind in the form of training is definitely better. Doing something for you on a regular basis makes Daisy feel useful and wanted, and provides her with the mental stimulation she needs.

Dogs thrive on a **regular routine** and the closer you can stick to that routine, the better. Frequent **variations** from her established schedule can **make** Daisy nervous and anxious and have **accidents in the house**, and can **create separation anxiety** when left alone. To the extent you can, adhere to a regular timetable and you will have a calm and happy dog.

You also need to recognize your dog's requirements for *physical exercise*. Taking Daisy out to the park on Saturday afternoon may not be enough for her. Many so-called behavior problems in dogs are the direct result of too little meaningful exercise and being cooped up too much. Just letting the dog out into the backyard or tying her to a line will not do. You need to get involved and participate. Under **no** circumstances let Daisy run loose on her own—not only is it usually illegal, dangerous for everyone around her and herself, but it goes against the entire concept and philosophy of being a Canine Good Citizen.

Good behavior requires good exercise, good company, good health, good nutrition and good training. **Good behavior requires YOU!**

WHEN TO START TRAINING

As soon as you bring your dog or puppy home, start training. Be consistent so that the dog learns only what you want it to know. Your puppy will learn, whether or not you train it. To prevent the dog from learning unwanted lessons, start training *now!*

Training begins as soon as you bring your puppy or dog home.

SUMMARY

1) The ideal time for bonding is from the forty-ninth to the eighty-fourth day.
2) Your dog is a social animal and needs companionship.
3) During the fear period, unpleasant experiences should be avoided.
4) It is easy to teach your dog to come when called *before* she has learned to run away.
5) In the development of her sense of identity, your dog may try to be the one in charge.
6) Start training your dog *now*.

4

Understanding
Your Dog

INSTINCTIVE BEHAVIORS, those our dogs have inherited from their ancestors and that are useful to us in the training process, can be grouped into three categories—**prey, pack** and **defense**—collectively called *drives*. Each one of these is governed by a basic trait.

Every dog is an individual who comes into the world with a specific grouping of genetically inherited, predetermined behaviors. How those behaviors are arranged, their intensity and how many component parts of each drive the dog has will determine temperament, personality, suitability for the task required and how the dog perceives the world.

BEHAVIORS IN EACH DRIVE

Prey drive includes those inherited behaviors associated with hunting, killing prey and feeding. It is *activated by motion, sound and smell*. Behaviors associated with prey drive are seeing, hearing,

Prey drive

Pack Drive

Defense Drive Fight

Flight

Prey, Pack and Defense drives.

scenting, tracking, stalking, chasing, pouncing, high-pitched barking, jumping up, biting, killing, pulling down, shaking, tearing and ripping apart, carrying, eating, digging and burying.

You see these behaviors when your dog is chasing a cat or gets excited and barks in a high-pitched tone of voice as the cat runs up a tree. Your dog may also shake and rip apart soft toys and bury dog biscuits in the couch.

Pack drive consists of behaviors associated with being part of a pack, including reproduction. Our dogs are social animals who evolved from the wolf. To hunt prey mostly larger than themselves, wolves have to live in a pack, which means adhering to a social hierarchy governed by strict rules of behavior to assure order. An ability to be part of a group and to fit in is important, and in the dog translates itself into a willingness to work with man as part of a team.

Pack drive is *stimulated by rank order in the social hierarchy.* Physical contact, playing and behaviors associated with social interaction with another dog—such as reading body language—as well as reproductive behaviors—such as licking, mounting, washing ears and all courting gestures—are part of Pack drive. The ability to breed and to be a good parent are also part of Pack drive.

A dog with many of these behaviors is the one that follows you around the house, is happiest when with you, loves to be petted and groomed and likes to work with you. The dog may be unhappy when left alone, which can express itself in separation anxiety.

Eliciting Prey Drive.

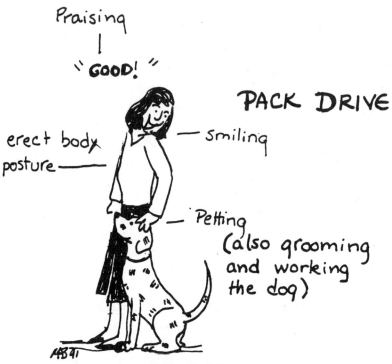

Praising
|
"GOOD!"

PACK DRIVE

erect body
posture

smiling

Petting
(also grooming
and working
the dog)

Eliciting Pack Drive.

Defense drive is governed by survival and self-preservation, and *consists of both fight and flight behaviors*. It is more complex because the same stimulus that can make a dog aggressive *(fight)*, can also elicit avoidance *(flight)* behaviors, especially in the young dog.

Fight behaviors tend not to be fully developed until the dog is over two years of age, although tendencies toward these behaviors will be seen at an earlier age. It can be observed in Bully, the dog that "stands tall," stares at other dogs and likes to "strut his stuff." Bully will stand his ground or go toward unfamiliar things, guard his food, toys or territory from other dogs or people and may dislike being petted or groomed. Bully is the one that will lie in front of doorways or cupboards, and his owner walks around Bully because he won't move on his own. These are all Defense drive *(fight)* behaviors.

Flight behaviors demonstrate that the dog is unsure. Hackles that go up the full length of the body—not just at the neck—hiding or running away from a new situation, a dislike of being touched

Eliciting Defense Drive.

by strangers or a general lack of confidence are all flight behaviors. Freezing (not going forward or backward) can be interpreted as inhibited flight behavior.

PERSONALITY PROFILE FOR DOGS

To help us understand how to approach each individual dog's training, we catalogued ten behaviors in each drive that influence the dog's responses and were useful to us in training, and created the Personality Profile. The ten behaviors chosen are those that most closely represent the strengths of the dog in each of the drives. The Profile does not pretend to include all behaviors seen in a dog or the complexity of their interaction.

The results of the Profile will give you a good starting point for tailoring a training program to your dog's needs. You can then make use of its strengths, avoid needless confusion and greatly reduce the time it takes to train the dog.

Evaluating the Profile

When completing the Profile, keep in mind that it was devised for a house dog or pet with an enriched environment, perhaps even a little training, and not a dog tied out or kept solely in a kennel— such dogs have fewer opportunities to express as many behaviors as a house dog. Answers should indicate those behaviors Daisy would

47

exhibit if she had not already been trained to do otherwise. For example, did she jump on people or the counter to steal food before she was trained not to do so? Other behaviors are, in turn, only seen in a training context, for example, during distraction training.

The fight part of the Defense drive does not fully express itself until the dog is mature, around two to four years of age, depending on the breed, although tendencies toward those behaviors may be seen earlier. Young dogs tend to exhibit more flight behaviors than older dogs.

Now What?

Before you can use the results of the Profile, you first have to take a look at what you are trying to teach Daisy and which drive she has to be in to perform a given exercise correctly.

All of the exercises for the Canine Good Citizen require Daisy to be in Pack drive. For these exercises you certainly don't want your dog to be in Prey *(chase)*, or Defense drives *(guard or flee)*. All else being equal, a dog with many Pack behaviors (more than sixty) will have no difficulty with learning these exercises.

Prey drive behaviors, those required for retrieving and jumping, although not necessary for the Canine Good Citizen test, come in handy in the *training* of the dog that has few Pack behaviors. Through the use of a treat or toy, you can exploit prey behaviors to *teach* a pack exercise.

Theoretically, dogs do not need Defense drive (fight) behaviors for the Canine Good Citizen test, but the *absence* of these behaviors has important ramifications. It is pivotal and determines how the dog has to be trained.

The beauty of the drives theory, if used correctly, is that it gives us a tool to overcome areas where a dog is weak. For example, it can be used to teach a dog with *few* Pack behaviors how to walk on a loose leash by using Prey behaviors.

BRINGING OUT DRIVES

Following are the basic rules for bringing out drives:
1. **Prey** drive is elicited by the use of motion—hand signals (except Stay), a high-pitched tone of voice or an object of

attraction (stick, ball or food), chasing or being chased and leaning backward with your body.

2. **Pack** drive is elicited by touching, praising and smiling at the dog. Grooming, playing and training with your body erect all bring out Pack drive behaviors.

3. **Defense** drive behavior is elicited by leaning over the dog, either from the front or the side, checking (a sharp tug on the leash), a harsh tone of voice and use of the Stay hand signal.

SWITCHING DRIVES

Daisy can instantaneously switch herself from one drive to another. Picture her playing with her favorite toy (Prey), when the doorbell rings. She drops the toy and starts to bark (Defense). You open the door and it is a neighbor whom Daisy knows. She goes to greet the visitor (Pack) and returns to play with her toy (Prey).

During training our task is to figure out how to switch the dog from one drive into another. For example, you are teaching Daisy to walk on a loose leash in the yard when a rabbit pops out of the hedge. She spots it, runs to the end of the leash, straining and barking excitedly in a high-pitched voice. She is in full Prey drive. Now you have to get her back into Pack where she needs to be in order to walk at your side. To get Daisy from Prey into Pack, you first have to go through Defense, at least in the teaching process and until the dog has learned to do it herself.

Volhard
Canine Personality Profile

When presented with the opportunity, does your dog (name) _____

Always - 10	Sometimes - 5	Never - 0

1) Sniff the ground or air a lot? _____

2) Get along with other dogs? _____

3) Stand his/her ground or investigate strange objects or sounds? _____

4) Run away from new situations? _____

49

5) Get excited by moving objects, such as bikes or squirrels? ____

6) Get along with people? ____

7) Like to play tug-of-war games to win? ____

8) Hide behind you when he/she can't cope? ____

9) Stalk cats, other dogs or things in the grass? ____

10) Bark when left alone? ____

11) Bark or growl in a deep tone? ____

12) Act fearful in unfamiliar situations? ____

13) When excited, bark in a high-pitched voice? ____

14) Solicit petting, or like to snuggle with you? ____

15) Guard territory? ____

16) Tremble or whine when unsure? ____

17) Pounce on toys? ____

18) Like to be groomed? ____

19) Guard food or toys? ____

20) Crawl or turn upside down when reprimanded? ____

21) Shake and "kill" toys? ____

22) Seek eye contact with you? ____

23) Dislike being petted? ____

24) Avoid coming close to you when called? ____

25) Steal food or garbage? ____

26) Follow you around like a shadow? ____

27) Guard his/her owner(s)? ____

28) Have difficulty standing still when groomed? ____

29) Like to carry things? ____

30) Play a lot with other dogs? ____

31) Dislike being groomed or bathed? ____

32) Cringe when someone strange bends over him/her? ____

33) Wolf down food? ____

34) Jump up to greet people? ____

35) Like to fight other dogs? ____

36) Urinate during greeting behavior? ____

37) Like to dig and bury things? ____

38) Show reproductive behaviors, such as courting or mounting other dogs? ____

39) When a young dog, get picked on by other dogs? ____

40) Tend to bite when cornered? ____

The precise manner in which you get Daisy back into Pack—remember, you must go through Defense—depends on the strength of her Defense drive. If she has a large number of Defense (fight) behaviors, you can give her a firm tug on the leash (check), which

Switching from Prey into Pack, through Defense.

switches her out of Prey into Defense. To get her into Pack, touch her gently on the top of the head, smile at her and tell her how clever she is and continue to work on walking on a loose leash. If she is low in Defense (fight) behaviors, a check may overpower her, and a voice communication such as "Ah, ah" will be sufficient to put her out of Prey and into Defense, after which you put her into Pack drive.

For the dog that has few fight behaviors and a large number of flight behaviors, a check is often counterproductive. Body postures, such as bending over the dog, or a deep tone of voice are usually enough to elicit Defense drive. Your dog, by her response to your training—cowering, rolling upside down, not wanting to come to

Volhard

Canine Personality Profile

Scoring

Name of dog _____

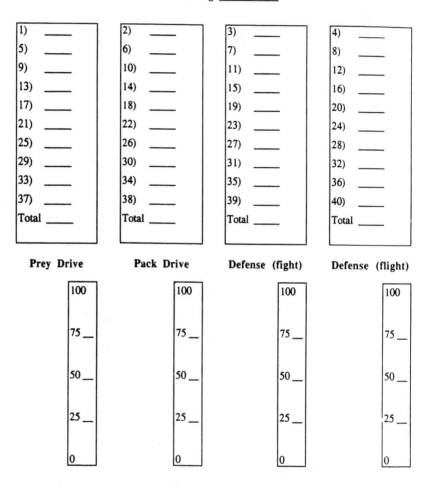

| Prey Drive | Pack Drive | Defense (fight) | Defense (flight) |

you for the training session—will show you when you overpower her, thereby making learning difficult, if not impossible.

The Basic Rules for Switching

1. From **Prey into Pack** in the teaching process, you go through Defense. How you put your dog into Defense will

Facial expression and body posture are inconsistent with the "Come" command and will confuse the dog.

depend on the number of Defense (fight) behaviors she has. As a general rule, the more Defense (fight) behaviors the dog has, the firmer the check needs to be.

As the dog learns, a barely audible voice communication or a slight change in body posture will suffice to encourage your dog to go from Prey through Defense into Pack drive. Once Daisy has learned what you want her to know, she switches herself.

2. From **Defense into Pack** by touching or smiling.
3. From **Pack into Prey** with an object (food) or motion.

Applying the concept of drives and learning which drive Daisy has to be in and how to get her there will speed up your training process enormously. You will no longer confuse Daisy. As you become aware of the impact your body stance and motions have on the drive she is in, your messages will be perfectly clear to your dog. Your body language is congruent with what you are trying to teach. Since Daisy is an astute observer of body motions (this is how dogs communicate with each other), she will understand exactly what you want.

PRACTICAL APPLICATION

By looking at your dog's profile, you will know which training techniques work best and are in harmony with your dog's drives. You now have the tools to tailor your training program for your dog.

Defense (fight)—more than 60. Your dog will not be bothered too much by a firm hand.

Body posture is not critical, although incongruent postures on your part will slow down the training. Tone of voice should be firm, but pleasant and nonthreatening.

Defense (flight)—more than 60. Your dog will not respond to force training and you will have to rely mainly on the other drives.

Correct body posture and quiet, pleasant tone of voice are critical. Avoid using a harsh tone of voice and any hovering, either leaning over or toward your dog. There is a premium on congruent body postures and gentle handling.

Prey—more than 60. Your dog will respond well to the use of a treat or toy during the teaching phase. A firm hand may be necessary, depending on the strength of the Defense drive (fight) to suppress the Prey drive when in high gear, such as when chasing a cat or spotting a squirrel. These dogs are easily motivated, but also easily distracted by motion or moving objects.

Signals will mean more to this dog than commands. There is a premium on using body, hands and leash correctly so as not to confuse the dog.

Prey—less than 60. Your dog is probably not easily motivated by food or other objects, but is also not easily distracted by moving objects.

Pack—more than 60. Your dog responds readily to praise and touch, likes to be with you and will respond with little guidance.

Pack—less than 60. Start praying. Daisy probably does not care whether she is with you or not. She likes to do her own thing and is not easily motivated. Your only hope is to rely on Prey drive in training. Limited Pack drive is usually breed-specific for dogs bred to work independently of man.

Dogs that exhibit an overabundance of Prey or Pack are also easily trained, but you will have to pay more attention to the strengths of their drives and exploit those behaviors most useful to you in training. You now have the tools to do it!

Important hint: If your dog is high in Defense (fight), you need to work especially diligently on—and review frequently—your leadership exercises, described in Chapter 1. If your dog is high in Prey, you also need to work on these exercises, not necessarily because your dog wants to become pack leader, but to control her around doorways and moving objects. If your dog is high in both, you may need professional help.

Art Clogg from Fredericton, New Brunswick, Canada, has come up with the following nicknames for some profiles:

The Couch Potato—low Prey, low Pack, low Defense. Difficult to motivate and probably does not need any training. Needs extra patience if training is attempted since there are few behaviors with which to work. On the plus side, this dog is unlikely to get into trouble, will not disturb anyone, will make a good family pet and does not mind being left alone for considerable periods of time.

The Hunter—high Prey, low Pack, low Defense. This dog will give the appearance of having an extremely short attention span, but is perfectly able to concentrate on what it finds interesting. Training will require the channeling of her energy to get the dog to do what you want. Patience will be required because the dog will have to be taught through Prey drive.

The Gas Station Dog—high Prey, low Pack, high Defense (fight). This dog is independent and not easy to live with as a pet and companion. Highly excitable by movement and may attack anything that comes within range. Does not care much about people or dogs and will do well as a guard dog. Pack exercises such as heeling need to be built up through prey. A real challenge.

The Runner—high Prey, low Pack, high Defense (flight). Easily startled and/or frightened. Needs quiet and reassuring handling. Not a good choice for children.

The Shadow—low Prey, high Pack, low Defense. This dog will follow you around all day and it is doubtful that she will get into trouble. Likes to be with you and is not interested in chasing much of anything.

Teacher's Pet—medium (50–75) Prey, Pack and Defense (fight). Easy to train and motivate. Mistakes on your part are not critical.

At our training camps and seminars we have the owners put the profile of their dogs in graph form for easy "reading." The graph for Teacher's Pet looks like this:

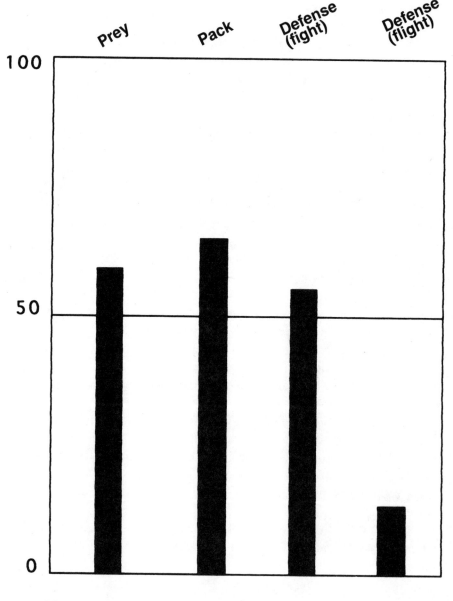

Profile at a Glance

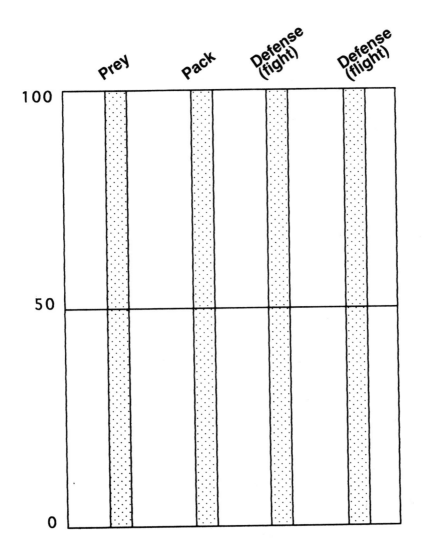

By now you have gathered that the easiest dogs are those that are balanced among all drives. No matter what you do, the dog seems to be able to figure out what you want. If you are lucky enough to have a dog like that, take good care of her. By applying the principles of drives, she will do well by you.

Use the graph above and you have your dog's profile "at a glance."

SUMMARY

1) Prey drive is elicited by motion, sounds and odors.
2) Pack drive is elicited by an inviting body posture, touching and a friendly voice.
3) Defense drive is elicited by a threatening body posture, hitting and an unfriendly voice.
4) The dog can switch at will on his/her own from one drive to another.
5) To switch the dog from Prey into Pack drive the owner must go through defense.
6) Your dog's profile tells you the correct way to train.

5

Stress and Your Dog

STRESS IS DEFINED as the body's response to any physical or mental demand. The response prepares the body to either *fight or flee*. It increases blood pressure, heart rate, breathing and metabolism, and there is a marked increase in the blood supply to the arms and legs. It is a physiological, genetically predetermined reaction over which the individual, whether it is a dog or a person, has no control.

When stressed, the body becomes chemically unbalanced. To deal with this imbalance the body releases chemicals into the bloodstream in an attempt to rebalance itself. The reserve of these chemicals is limited. You can dip into it only so many times before it runs dry and the body loses its ability to rebalance. Prolonged periods of imbalance result in neurotic behavior and the inability to function.

Mental or physical stress ranges from tolerable all the way to intolerable—that is, the inability to function. Our interest here deals with stress experienced during training, whether we are teaching a new exercise or practicing a familiar one, or during the test. We want you to be able to recognize the signs of stress and to know what you can do to manage the stress your dog may experience.

Only then can you prevent stress from adversely affecting your dog's performance during your training and the Canine Good Citizen test itself.

POSITIVE AND NEGATIVE STRESS— MANIFESTATIONS

Stress is characterized as "positive"—manifesting itself in **in**creased activity—and "negative"—manifesting itself in **de**creased activity. Picture yourself returning home after a hard day at work. You are welcomed by a mess on the brand-new white living room carpet. What is your response? Do you explode, scream at poor Max, your spouse, the children and then storm through the house slamming doors? Or do you look at the mess in horror, shake

Example of "**positive**" stress.

your head in resignation, feel drained of energy, ignore the dog, the spouse and the children and retire to your room?

In the first example, your body was energized by the chemicals released into the bloodstream. In the second example, your body was debilitated.

Dogs react in a similar manner and stress triggers the fight/flight response. **Positive stress** manifests itself in hyperactivity, such as running around, bouncing up and down or jumping on you, whining, barking, mouthing, getting in front of you or anticipating commands. You may think your dog is just being silly and tiresome, but for the dog those are coping behaviors.

Negative stress manifests itself by lethargy, such as freezing, slinking behind you, running away or responding slowly to a command. In new situations, Max seems tired and wants to lie down, or he seems sluggish and disinterested. These are not signs of relaxation, but are the coping behaviors for negative stress.

Example of "**negative**" stress.

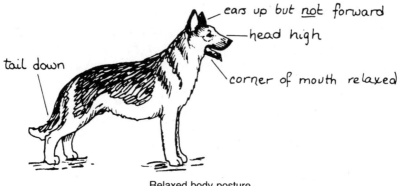

ears up but __not__ forward

—head high

tail down

corner of mouth relaxed

Relaxed body posture.

Signs of either form of stress are muscle tremors, excessive panting or drooling, sweaty feet that leave tracks on dry, hard surfaces, dilated pupils and, in extreme cases, urination or defecation—usually in the form of diarrhea—and self-mutilation. Behaviors such as pushing into you or going in front of or behind you during distraction training are stress-related.

Stress is a normal part of our lives and it is the little stresses that go on every day that add to the wear and tear of the body, the mess on the rug being the last straw. It becomes the threshold beyond which you can no longer concentrate or function normally, and thereby become anxious.

Anxiety is a state of apprehension, uneasiness. When it is prolonged, two things happen. First, the ability to learn and to think clearly is diminished and ultimately stops. It can also cause a panic attack. Second, it depresses the immune system, thereby increasing our chances of becoming physically ill. It affects our dogs in the same way. The weakest link in the chain is attacked first. If the dog has structural flaws, such as weak pasterns, he may begin to limp or show signs of pain. Digestive upsets are another common reaction to stress.

Stress, in and of itself, is not anything bad or undesirable. A certain level of stress is vital for the development and healthy functioning of the body and its immune system. It is only when there is no behavioral outlet for stress—when the dog is put in a no-win situation—that the burden of coping is born by the body and the immune system starts to break down.

62

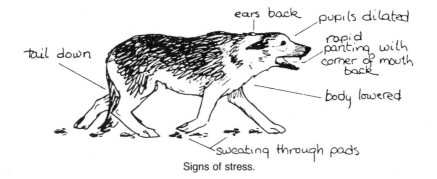

ears back · pupils dilated

rapid panting with corner of mouth back

tail down

body lowered

sweating through pads

Signs of stress.

SOURCES OF STRESS—INTRINSIC AND EXTRINSIC

Sources of stress are intrinsic or extrinsic. **Intrinsic** sources are all the things that come with the dog, including structure and health. They are inherited and come from within the dog. Dogs vary in coping abilities and stress thresholds, and what you see is what you get. Realistically, there is not much you can do to change your

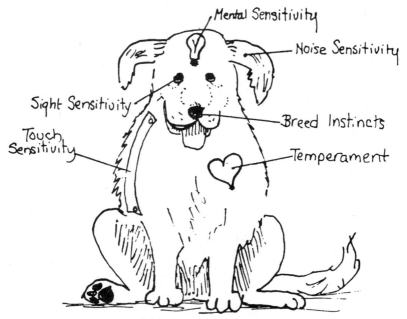

Mental Sensitivity

Noise Sensitivity

Sight Sensitivity

Touch Sensitivity

Breed Instincts

Temperament

Intrinsic sources of stress.

63

Extrinsic sources of stress.

dog, such as training a dog to deal better with stress. You can use stress-management techniques to mitigate the impact of stress.

Extrinsic sources range from the diet you feed to even the relationship you have with your dog. They come from outside the dog and are introduced externally. Extrinsic sources include lack of adequate socialization, appropriateness of the training method being used, the location where the training takes place, frustration and indecision on your part and how the dog perceives its environment. Fortunately, *all these are under your control.*

STRESS AND LEARNING

All learning is stressful. For many, ourselves included, one of the most recent learning experiences was brought on by the computer revolution. In our case, there were plenty of times during the learning process when we were tempted to throw the

Stress creates anxiety.

agonizing contraption out the window. At that moment, learning and the ability to think rationally had stopped. There was no point in trying to go on until the body had the chance to rebalance itself.

When you train Max, you cannot prevent him from experiencing some stress, but you can keep it at a level where he can still learn. Recognize the signs of stress and when you should stop. When Max reaches the point where he can no longer learn, whatever he does will be the result of random, redirected or displacement behaviors and will not be committed to memory. Even though he may respond to the command, his anxiety level will be such that he will not retain what you are trying to teach him.

There are going to be times when Max just doesn't get the message. It can happen at any time, especially when you are working with distractions. Nothing you do works and you feel you are not making any progress.

"What can I do?" people often ask. "If I stop, Max will think he has won and he will never do it for me." This argument is completely without merit because it presumes that you and Max are adversaries, in some kind of a contest, such as, "You will do it no

When your dog stresses, it's time to take a break.

matter what." If you approach training with this attitude, you are doomed to failure; at best, you will have an unrewarding relationship with your dog.

Training Max has nothing to do with *winning*, but everything to do with *teaching*. You can walk away from a training session at any time, whether or not you think you have been successful. When you see that no further learning is taking place, stop! If you don't and insist on forcing the issue, you will undermine your dog's trust in you and the relationship you are trying to build.

Let Max rest for several hours and try again. You will find that all of a sudden the lightbulb seems to have gone on. By having taken a break at that point, you give latent learning—the process of getting the point through time—a chance to work.

Our advice is to quit training when you find yourself becoming irritable or when Max starts to show signs of severe stress.

Konrad Most, the "father" of training as we know it today, recognized the importance of maintaining the dog's equilibrium. In his 1910 training manual he wrote, "Good training needs a kind heart as well as a cool and well-informed head. . . ." Anyone can dominate a dog by physical or mental pressure, but only through the building of confidence by positive reinforcement can reliability and enjoyment of performance be achieved. Max must perceive you as trustworthy or he will begin to exhibit neurotic behaviors.

STRESS AND DISTRACTION TRAINING

When distractions are introduced in training, your dog may not respond as you expected. As a result, you may become a little frustrated, taking the attitude ''How could you do this to me?'' Max senses your feelings and becomes apprehensive and anxious. He only understands you are upset, but does not understand why. Unless you now calm yourself *and* him, and reassure him that he is a good boy and should keep trying, your training session will deteriorate to the point where all learning stops.

When you take your Canine Good Citizen test, it is especially important for you to remain calm and control any nervousness you may experience, because your dog is acutely aware of your emotions, which are likely to interfere with his performance. Remember,

Your nervousness will affect your dog.

67

the object of the training and the test is to make both positive experiences for you and your dog.

Most of the tests for the Canine Good Citizen involve some form of distraction or another. You will need to monitor your dog's reaction to these distractions so you can help him cope. One test requires you to be out of your dog's sight for five minutes, which can be a source of significant stress to your dog. You will need to introduce him to and condition him for this exercise in such a way that any stress he may experience is minimized.

The first impression leaves the most lasting impact. Whenever you introduce your dog to a new exercise or distraction, make it as pleasant and as stress-free as possible so that it leaves a neutral, if not favorable, impression.

STRESS MANAGEMENT

Become aware of *how* Max reacts to stress, that is, positively or negatively, and the *circumstances* under which he stresses. It could be a location or something you are doing.

Let's say Max *stresses* in a *"positive"* way, which means he gets overexcited and bouncy. In the case of a person, we would say he or she is hysterical. In old movies, when someone started scream-ing uncontrollably, this was handled by slapping the person on the cheek. For Max, a check on the collar to settle him down would be the same thing. Keep your hands still and *off* your dog, and your voice quiet, or you will excite him even more. Give him the Down command and enforce it. Every behavior has a time frame and experience will tell you how long it takes Max to calm down under different circumstances. During times of severe stress, Max is unable to learn or respond to commands, even those he knows well, until his body rebalances itself. Your goal is to restore Max's breathing pattern and body posture to normal.

If Max *stresses* in a *"negative"* way, take him for a *walk* to get the circulation going and redistribute the chemicals that have been released, so his breathing can return to normal. *Massage* the top of his shoulders to relax him—just because he is quiet does not mean he is calm. Try to turn him on with an object or food. Under **no** circumstances should you use a check to get him "out of it." It will produce even greater lethargy.

Understand that Max has *no control* over his response to stress—he *inherited* this behavior—and that it is *your* job to manage it as best as you can. Through proper management, Max will become accustomed, with every successful repetition, to coping with new situations and handle them like an old trooper.

SUMMARY

1) Learn how your dog stresses—in a "positive" or "negative" way.
2) Sources of stress are intrinsic—from sources within the dog—and extrinsic—from sources outside the dog.
3) Stress creates a chemical imbalance in the body.
4) Only *you* can manage the stress your dog feels during training.
5) When your dog does not respond as expected, stay calm and try again.
6) Should your dog stress beyond the ability to learn during training, stop and give his physical system a chance to rebalance.

Bean before the Sit.

6

Sit! Down! Stand! Stay!

IN THIS CHAPTER we are going to show you how to train Max to do the Sit, Down and Stand, and to remain in position on command. Four of the ten tests require Max to remain in position, or "Stay," so you can see this command is important. For the Canine Good Citizen you only need the Sit and the Down, but we think it's a good idea to teach Max the Stand as well. Knowing this exercise certainly makes grooming and visits to the veterinarian a lot easier.

TEACHING THE SIT

We have chosen the Sit as your introduction to training your dog for two reasons: First, because it is the simplest of the exercises to teach; and second, because it is one of the most practical.

For example, one question owners frequently ask is "How do I keep my dog from jumping on people?" Dogs jump on people as a form of greeting, like saying "Hello, nice to meet you!" As annoying as it may be at times, please remember that it is a gesture of affection and goodwill, which is why we do not recommend any form of punishment to deal with it.

So how do you stop Max from jumping up on you, family members or friends without undermining the relationship you are trying to build? By teaching him to Sit and Stay on command. He can't jump on you or anybody else when he is sitting—the two behaviors are mutually exclusive.

Equally annoying, but far more dangerous is the dog's habit of dashing through doors just because they are open. It is dangerous because Max may find himself in the middle of the road and get run over, or if you are in the process of opening a door, he may knock you down as he rushes through. Such potential accidents can be prevented if you teach your dog to Sit and Stay while you open the door and until you release him with "OK."

The same applies to going up or down stairs, as well as getting in and out of the car. Similarly, when the doorbell rings, you can tell Max "Sit" and "Stay" while you answer it instead of having him frantically charge the door. All these maneuvers can be performed smoothly and without worry, once you have taught Max to Sit and Stay on command. It gives you a wonderfully easy way to control him when you need it most.

Commands to Be Taught

You are going to teach Max three commands:

1. Sit
2. Stay
3. OK

OK is the release word and means he no longer has to stay. Make it a strict rule that once you have told Max to "Stay," you must release him. Should you get lax or lazy about releasing Max, he will get into the habit of releasing himself. That will teach him *he* can decide when to move, the very opposite of what you want him to learn.

Unless impaired, a dog's sense of hearing is extremely acute and *when giving a command there is absolutely no need to shout.* Commands are given in a normal tone of voice, such as "Sit."

Prevent this with Sit and Stay.

Teaching the Sit. *Photo by Jack Volhard*

"Sit!" is a command; it is **not** "Sit?" **the question**. The release word "OK" is given in a more excited tone of voice, to convey "That's it, you're all done for now."

When teaching a new command, you may have to repeat it several times before your dog catches on. Once past that initial stage, teach Max to respond to the *first* command. Give the command and if nothing happens, show your dog exactly what it is you want by physically helping him. Consistency is the key to success. During the Canine Good Citizen test you are permitted to talk to your dog and give more than one command.

Teaching Your Dog to Sit on Command

Your dog already knows how to sit. What he has to learn is what you expect from him when you say "Sit." Max must also learn to obey every time you give him the command. When you train Max, be sure he is wearing his collar just in case you need it for extra control.

Begin by standing in front of Max, showing him a small, bite-sized treat or a toy that catches his attention, holding it just a little in front of his eyes, slightly over his head. Say "Sit" as you bring

74

Teaching the Sit with your hand through collar for a large dog.

Photo by Jack Volhard

your hand above his eyes. Looking up at the treat will cause Max to sit. When he does, give him the treat and tell him what a good puppy he is. Tell him without petting him. If you pet as you praise him, he will probably get up when you really want him to focus on sitting. Count to ten and release him with ''OK.'' From the beginning introduce Max to the release word and insist that he wait in position until you say it's OK to move.

Study the illustration on page 74 for the position of your hand in relation to your dog's head. If your hand is held too high, your dog will jump up; if it is too low, he will not sit.

If Max is low in Prey drive—less than 40—he may not respond to the treat or toy. You will have to physically place him. With Max at your left side and both of you facing in the same direction, place your right hand against his chest and your left hand on his shoulder. With your left hand stroke down the entire length of his back, over the tail all the way to his stifles, and with equal pressure of the right and left hands, fold him into a Sit with "Sit." When he sits, praise enthusiastically with "Good boy," keeping your hands in position. Concentrate on keeping your hands still—no petting—count to ten and release Max with "OK." If Max is too large or too bouncy for you to perform this maneuver, put your hand through the collar at the top of his neck between the ears, and sit him by pulling up on the collar with your right hand and folding his hind legs with your left.

For all service and working activities—American Kennel Club competitive events, Guide Dogs for the Blind, Canine Corps, etc.—traditionally the dog is on the handler's left side. Even though the dog can be either on the left or the right for the Canine Good Citizen test, we recommend that you train Max on your left just in case you want to pursue other training activities. Practice the Sit with Max five times in a row for five days.

When Max understands what "Sit" means, you can start to teach him to obey your command. Put two or more fingers of your right hand through the collar at the top of his neck, palm facing up, and tell him to "Sit." If he does, give him a treat and tell him how good he is; if he does not, pull up on his collar and wait until he sits, then praise and reward him with a treat.

How to Reward

Practice until Max Sits on command, that is, without you having to pull up on the collar, and then without having to touch it. Give a treat and praise with "Good puppy" for *every* correct response.

When he Sits on command *only*, reward the desired response every other time. Finally, reward him on a random basis—every now and then give him a treat after he has sat on command. A random reward is the most powerful reinforcement of what your dog has learned. It is based on the simple premise that hope springs eternal. To make it work, all you have to do is use it and keep using it!

Now when Max wants to greet you by jumping up, tell him "sit." Bend down, briefly pet him and tell him what a good puppy he is, then release him. By following this simple method consistently, you will have changed your dog's greeting behavior from trying to jump on you to sitting to be petted, which is one of the Canine Good Citizen tests.

You are now ready to teach Max to remain in position with the command "Stay."

TEACHING YOUR DOG TO STAY

This exercise is taught on leash. Arrange Max's collar so that the ring for the leash is at the top of his neck, between his ears, and attach the leash to the collar. Put the loop end of the leash over your right thumb, and with your left hand fold the excess back and forth, accordion style, into your right hand. This way, the part of the leash attached to the dog comes out from under your little finger. Grasp the leash with your left hand, palm facing you, and place both hands comfortably against your thighs.

With Max sitting at your left side, both of you facing in the same direction, transfer the leash from the right into the left hand, thumb pointing up and leash coming out the bottom of your hand to the dog's collar. Hold your left hand above Max's neck with slight tension on the collar. Say and signal "Stay." The Stay signal is given with your right hand in a pendulum motion coming across your body to a point in front of Max's nose. Return your hand to your right side. Take a step to the right, silently count to ten, step back, release tension and quietly praise your dog (no hands). Praise is not the same as the release and it is not an invitation to move. If Max gets up when you praise, put him back and start all over.

Repeat, and this time step directly in front. After counting to ten, step back, release tension, praise, pause and release. Incorporate the Stay exercise into your training routine. Your goal is a thirty-second Sit-Stay with you directly in front of your dog at the end of five days.

When you and Max are ready to progress to the next sequence, arrange the collar with the rings under Max's chin, hold the leash in your left hand, say and signal "Stay" and go three feet in front. There is no tension on the leash and no more than a half-inch of slack. Place the left hand at your belt buckle and your right hand at your side. Count to ten, return, praise, pause and release.

How to hold the leash in the control position.   *Photo by Jack Volhard*

Should Max try to move or think about moving, step toward him on your right foot and slap up on the leash with your right hand to a point directly above his head with "Stay." How do you know when Max is thinking about moving? By observing him during your training it will not take you long to interpret his thoughts. As a rule of thumb, whenever he is not looking at you, he is probably thinking of moving. Also, watch his thigh muscles—they will visibly contract just as he is about to get up. Over the course of five sessions gradually build up the time you stand in front of Max from ten seconds to one minute.

Repeat this exercise standing 6 feet in front of your dog. Should

The "Stay" hand signal.   *Photo by Jack Volhard*

Max move, put him back without saying anything. When you see
that he is steady, over the course of several sessions gradually
increase the distance you leave Max to 20 feet for thirty seconds.

For the Canine Good Citizen test, you will have to put Max
on a 20-foot line, walk forward the length of the line, turn around
and return to your dog at a natural pace. You may leave the dog in
either a Sit or a Down-Stay. Although Max does *not* have to *maintain*
the position in which you left him, he *must* remain *in place*. Still,
we think it preferable to teach your dog to remain in position. Once
Max gets the idea that it's OK to change position, he may also get
the idea that it's OK to wander off.

SAFETY EXERCISES

We consider it unacceptable to have dogs bolting through doors, out of cars or up and down stairs. It is not only annoying, but also is dangerous for you and your dog. Get into the habit of having your dog sit and stay before you open *any* door. Some of us prefer to go through the doorway first, while others want the dog to go through first. It makes no difference, so long as *Max stays until you release him*. Practice with doors the dog uses regularly, including car doors. Each time you make your dog Sit and Stay it reinforces your position as pack leader and the one in charge.

If you have stairs, start teaching your dog to stay at the bottom while you go up. First sit him and give the Stay command. When he tries to follow, put him back and start again. Practice until you can go all the way up the stairs while the dog waits at the bottom before you release him to follow. Repeat the same procedure going down the stairs.

Once your dog has been trained to wait at one end of the stairs, you will discover that he will anticipate the release. He will "jump the gun" and get up just as you are about to release him. Before long, he will only stay briefly and release when *he* chooses. It may happen almost as soon as he has grasped the idea or it may take a few weeks or even months, but it *will* happen.

When it does, stop whatever you are doing and put him back, count to ten and release him. *Do not let him get into the habit of releasing himself.* Consistency is just as important here as it is teaching any other exercise.

TEACHING THE DOWN

For the Canine Good Citizen test you will have to demonstrate that Max will lie Down on command. This exercise can be taught together with the Sit on command.

First, sit your dog at your left side, both of you facing in the same direction. Put two fingers of your left hand, palm facing you, through the collar at the side of the dog's neck. Have a treat in your right hand. Show the treat and lower it straight down and in front of your dog as you apply downward pressure on the collar, at the

Teaching your dog to lie Down on command.   *Photos by Jack Volhard*

81

same time saying "Down." When he lies down, give the treat and praise by saying what a good puppy he is. Keep your left hand in the collar and your right hand off the dog while telling Max how clever he is so that he learns that this praise is for lying down. If Max is a small dog you may want to put him on a table for this exercise to save your back.

Reverse the process by showing a treat and bringing it up slightly above Max's head with upward pressure on the collar as you give the command "Sit." Look at the illustration on page 00 and study the way the right hand moves down and in front of your dog in an "L" shape, as well as the position of the left hand. **Hint:** Place the treat between your dog's front legs and then slide it forward.

Practice having your dog lie down at your side five times in a row for five days, or until he does it on command with *minimal* pressure on the collar. Praise and reward with a treat *every time*.

If Max does not respond to the treat, physically place him into the Down position as follows:

- Kneel next to your sitting dog, both of you facing in the same direction.
- Drape your left arm across Max's shoulder so that your hand, palm up, is behind his left foreleg, just below the elbow.
- Place your right hand behind his right foreleg.
- Holding your dog's forelegs in your palms, lift him into the begging position and lower him to the ground with "Down."
- Praise quietly while keeping your hands still and in position.
- Count to ten and release your dog.

It is important that when you lift Max into the begging position that your thumbs are up or folded into your palms and that you do not apply pressure on his forelegs with your thumbs. If you squeeze the forelegs, your dog will try to pull his legs away and you may wind up in a wrestling match, thereby making the exercise needlessly frightening for Max.

When he understands what the word means, you can move on to the next step. Sit your dog at your left side and put two fingers of your left hand through the collar, palm facing you, at the side of his neck. Say "Down" and apply downward pressure on the collar. When he lies down, praise and give a treat. Practice over the course

Reinforcing the Down command.   *Photos by Jack Volhard*

of several days until Max will lie Down on command without any pressure on the collar. After that, when he lies Down on command, *randomly reward* as explained above.

The procedure for teaching the Down-Stay is the same as for the Sit-Stay.

For the Canine Good Citizen test you have two options for this exercise. One is to have Max stand at your side, tell him "Sit" and then tell him "Down." You then do the 20-foot Stay with Max in the Down position. It is this sequence which is generally the easiest *provided* Max is standing at the start or you can readily get him to stand. The other option is to start with Max sitting at your side, telling him "Down" and then "Sit," followed by the 20-foot Stay with Max in the sitting position.

Whichever option you find easier to teach, *remember that Max has to respond to your commands*. You may repeat a command and use a signal as well, but you *may not* force Max into either position. Although you are allowed to touch the dog to "offer gentle guidance," we suggest that you keep your hands off Max during this exercise so that whatever guidance you give him can't be misconstrued as force by the evaluator.

TEACHING THE STAND

Although the Stand is not a requirement for the Canine Good Citizen test, we have included it in this chapter because it is such a valuable exercise to teach your dog. It is certainly a lot easier brushing, grooming and wiping feet, as well as visiting the veterinarian, with a dog that has been trained to stand still rather than with one that is in perpetual motion.

Depending on the size of your dog, you should either stand, kneel on your left or both knees or have the dog on a table. What you want to avoid is looming over him, because if you do, he will want to move away from you, especially if he is low in Defense (fight) drive.

Start with Max sitting at your left side, off leash, both of you facing in the same direction with your shoulders square and not turned toward him. Put the thumb of your right hand in the collar under his chin, fingers pointing to the floor, palm open and

Teaching your dog to Stand on command.   *Photos by Jack Volhard*

flat against his chest. Say "Stand" and at the same time apply backward pressure on his stifles with the back of your left hand. Keep both hands still and in place. Count to ten, praise and release.

When you put Max into a Stand, watch his front feet—they should remain in place and not move forward. Practice keeping Max standing still for one minute, once a training session, for five days. When he moves, readjust him. You can practice this exercise at the same time you work on the Sit and the Down.

When Max is steady *with* your hands holding him, the next step is to remove your left hand from his stifles after you have stood him. Then have Max stand for one minute.

After that, stand up, but keep your right hand on his chest and your shoulders square. The last step is to stand Max and take *both hands off* and have him do the Stand still for one minute with you at his side.

TRAINING SCHEDULE

Week One

Sit

With treat and hand held slightly above your dog's head, say "Sit." Praise, give a treat, count to ten and release. *Alternative*—right hand against chest, left hand to the stifles, fold dog into a Sit. Practice five times per session for five days.

Down

With your dog sitting, put two fingers of your left hand through the collar at the side of the dog's neck, with a treat in your right hand. Lower treat to the ground with "Down." Praise, give treat, count to ten and release. *Alternative*—kneel next to your sitting dog, both of you facing in the same direction, and with your left hand pick up your dog's left foreleg. Remember to keep your thumbs up. With your right hand pick up the right foreleg; lift and lower your dog into the Down position with "Down." Practice five times per session for five days.

Learn to observe Max so you can tell . . .

. . . when to reinforce the Stay command.

Stand

Sitting next to the dog, both of you facing in the same direction, put the thumb of your right hand through the collar under your dog's chin, palm against his chest. Say "Stand" and apply backward pressure on stifles with the back of your left hand. Remember to keep your dog's front feet stationary. Practice once a session keeping Max standing still for one minute with your hands in place. Readjust as necessary. After one minute, praise, pause and release.

Week Two

Sit

Put two fingers of your left hand through the collar at the top of his neck and say "Sit." Praise, give treat, count to ten and release. If he does not do a Sit, pull up on the collar, wait until he sits, praise, give a treat, count to ten and release.

Stay

Put the collar ring on top of the dog's neck and attach the leash, then neatly fold it into your left hand. Sit your dog at your left side, both of you facing in the same direction. Apply slight upward tension on the collar, give a signal and say "Stay," take a step to the right, count to ten, step back, praise and release.

If he moves, put him back and start all over. Repeat, standing directly in front of your dog. Step back, praise and release. Pause briefly between praising and releasing so that your dog does not think he can get up after you praise. The goal after five days is thirty seconds with you in front of your dog without him moving.

Down

Sit your dog at your left side, both of you facing in the same direction, and put two fingers of your left hand through the collar at the side of his neck. Say "Down" and apply downward pressure on the collar. Praise, give a treat, count to ten and release.

Stand

Stand the dog and then remove your left hand from his stifles and have him Stand for one minute. Keep your shoulders square and make sure his front feet remain in place. If Max moves, readjust him. After one minute, praise, pause and release. Practice once per session.

Week Three

Sit

The goal for this week is to have the dog do a Sit *without* having to pull up or touch the collar. Praise, give a treat for every correct response, count to ten and release. Practice five times per session for five days.

Stay

With your dog sitting at your left side, collar ring under the dog's chin, leash neatly folded in your left hand, signal and say "Stay," go 3 feet in front and put your left hand against your belt buckle. Slap the leash and/or put your dog back, as necessary. Learn to reinforce the Stay while your dog is *thinking* about moving. Count to ten, return, praise, pause and release. Practice once per session, gradually increasing the time until you can stand in front of your dog for one minute at the end of five days.

You may also want to practice the Stay in the Down position. Start as you would for the Sit-Stay. Should he try to move, take a step toward your dog, slide your left hand down the leash to a point directly under his chin and apply downward pressure. If the dog gets up, put him back. Goal after five days: a one-minute Down-Stay.

Down

The goal this week is for the dog to do a Down on command *without* having to touch the collar. Praise, give a treat for every correct response, count to ten and release. Practice five times per session for five days.

Stand

Stand next to your sitting dog. Stand the dog and take both the left and the right hand off Max. Be prepared to steady him by putting your right hand against his chest and/or your left hand in front of the stifles. Keep your shoulders square and make sure his front feet remain in place. If Max moves, reposition him. After one minute, praise, pause and release. Practice once per session.

Week Four

Sit

Begin using random rewards for correct responses. The dog should respond on command, without you having to touch or even *reach* for the collar.

Stay

Go to the end of the leash in front of Max. For the first session count to ten and return, etc. Gradually increase the time until you can stand at the end of the leash for one minute after five sessions. Practice once a session for five days. Repeat for the Down-Stay.

Down

Begin using random rewards for correct responses. The dog should respond on command without you having to touch or *reach* for the collar.

Stand

Stand your dog, signal and say "Stay," count to ten, praise, pause and release. Then practice having the dog stand still for one minute, once a session for five days.

Weeks Five Through Eight

See Chapter 8, Training with Distractions.

Most of us would like to be able to walk our dog on a loose leash.

7

Out for a Walk

YOU WILL HAVE TO DEMONSTRATE, as part of the Canine Good Citizen test, that you are in control when walking your dog. Put another way, Daisy has to learn not to pull on the leash, and she must be on your side and in such position as to leave no doubt that her attention is on you. Further, to demonstrate that the dog has no difficulty moving about in pedestrian traffic, you and Daisy will have to walk around and pass close by to several persons—at least three, one of whom may have a dog—in order to show that she behaves in public places.

Even if you don't ordinarily take Daisy for walks, it is still a good idea to teach her some manners while on leash. For example, at least once a year you will have to take her to the veterinarian, and if you train Daisy to walk on leash, the visit will go much more smoothly than if she bounces off the end of the leash like a kangaroo.

Most of us want to be able to take our dog for a walk on leash and have him or her remain within the length of the leash without pulling. A leisurely stroll is an important daily routine, and for many dogs the only opportunity to get some fresh air.

LEASH TRAINING YOUR DOG

Before you can start the section on teaching your dog not to pull, you will need to get Daisy accustomed to wearing a collar and teach her to walk on a leash.

From your local pet supply store, buy an adjustable buckle collar of fabric or leather and a 6-foot canvas or nylon leash. Take your dog's neck measurement before you go. The collar should be snug, like a turtleneck sweater, high on the neck and *just behind the ears*, so that she cannot slip out of it. You will probably have to buy a bigger one as Daisy grows.

Fasten the collar around her neck and see what she does. Most dogs, even puppies, show little reaction to a collar. Some will scratch their neck at first, but as they become accustomed to wearing the collar, they quickly ignore it.

Once she is used to the collar, attach the leash and let her drag it around. You will need to supervise her so that you can rescue her in case the leash gets caught in something. When she ignores the leash, pick up the other end and follow her around. She will happily wander off wherever fancy takes her. Usually, all of this can be done in two to three brief sessions.

You are now ready to show Daisy where you want her to go. First use a treat and have her follow you, and then gently guide her with the leash telling her how clever she is. If you are training outside, use the treat to coax Daisy away from the house and the leash to guide her back toward the house. Before you know it, she will not only walk on the leash in your direction, but actually pull you along.

TEACHING YOUR DOG TO WALK ON A LOOSE LEASH

To prepare you for what to expect, briefly review Daisy's Personality Profile. If her Pack drive score is higher than any of the other scores and at least 60, this exercise will be easy to teach her. If her Prey drive score is higher than any of the others, smells and moving objects will easily distract her. To overcome her distractibility, you can use a treat to teach her to walk on a loose leash.

94

A note of caution: Some dogs get *too* excited about treats. In this case the use of treats in training becomes counterproductive. If you have such a dog, use treats sparingly, if at all. You are looking for a balance between control and motivation, and you will need to play this by ear.

You need a collar, a 6-foot canvas or nylon leash and treats. Choose a command—the customary one is ''[Dog's name], Heel.'' The name is used first to get Daisy's attention, followed by the command. After you have given the command, start to walk—*briskly. There is a direct relationship between your pace and how quickly Daisy will catch on.* Your pace needs to be fast enough, without actually running, to keep Daisy's attention on you. Walk as though you are late for an appointment.

Although for the Canine Good Citizen, you may have Daisy either on your right or your left, we recommend that you train her to walk on your left, the traditional side for all activities where dogs serve people, such as guiding the blind, police work, as well as AKC Obedience competition. While at this point in your training you may not have any interest in other training activities, one or the other may appeal to you in the future. If you train Daisy on the left, you will not have to retrain her later on.

The Halt

You will also need to decide what you want your dog to do when you come to a Halt. We recommend that you teach Daisy to Sit even though this is not a requirement for the CGC. Every time you come to a Halt, place her into a Sit, as described in Chapter 6, by placing your right hand against her chest, your left behind the stifles, folding her into a Sit with the command ''Sit.'' As you come to a Halt, place your right knee on the ground and sit Daisy in line with your left leg. When you place Daisy into a Sit, make sure that both of you are facing in the same direction and that you are not leaning or hovering over her.

Heeling

Take Daisy to an area without too many distractions, such as other people and dogs, especially loose dogs, and where you can walk in a circle about 30 feet in diameter.

95

How to teach your dog to walk on a loose leash.

With Daisy sitting at your left side, both of you facing in the same direction, put the full length of the leash over your right shoulder. The object is to keep your hands off the leash unless you have to bring Daisy back to your left side. Say "[Dog's name], Heel," and start to walk at a brisk pace, keeping your body erect. When Daisy is at your left side, tell her how clever she is. If she *starts* to get ahead of you, use your left or both hands to bring her back to your left side with a tug on the leash. Immediately let go of the leash and tell her how good she is and keep moving. If you are walking in a large circle, go in a clockwise direction so that Daisy is on the outside of the circle. Whenever Daisy stays at your left side without pulling or getting ahead of you, praise or give her a treat.

You will have to repeat this several times over the course of a few training sessions until she understands where you want her to be and that you don't want her to pull. Your initial goal is to be able to walk for ten steps without Daisy pulling on the leash. If you don't see any results after ten minutes, see the alternatives that follow.

Next, practice until you can walk her on a loose leash for thirty steps. When you come to a halt, place her into a Sit by pulling up on the collar with your left hand with "Sit." Then do sixty steps, and finally, complete the entire circle.

If Daisy is low in Pack drive, but medium to high in Prey drive, you can use a treat to teach her Heel. Before you try that you need to know how treats are used in training.

Inducing and **rewarding** are the two ways treats are used in training. *Inducing* means Daisy knows you have the treat, sees the treat and responds because of the treat. *Rewarding* means that Daisy is not sure you have the treat and responds because she hopes she may get a treat. You induce for a response you would like to get, and reward for a response you have gotten.

Of the two, a *reward* used on a *random basis* is a more powerful long-term training aid because the dog responds out of hope. When you induce, the dog responds to the treat and when he gets tired of them or you don't have one, he may not respond at all.

Neatly fold the leash accordion-style into your left hand, with the part going to the dog coming out the bottom of your hand, and place your left hand against your belt buckle. Hold the treat in your right hand, show it, say "Daisy, Heel," take several steps forward and give her the treat. Then sit her and start again. Keep her attention on you and keep her next to you with the treat. **Important:** The natural tendency of the handler is to rotate the upper part of the body as he or she shows the treat to the dog so that the left shoulder points backward. When this happens it confuses the dog because the body posture is incongruous with what you want the dog to do. Your body posture says "stay back" and the treat says "stay at my side." You need to concentrate on keeping your left shoulder facing *forward*.

Remember that you are using the treat to keep her at your side, so reward that behavior. If you wait until she sits, a common mistake, you are rewarding the Sit and not the Stay at your side.

Over the course of the next five sessions, increase the number of steps between starting and stopping in two-step increments, until you can walk thirty steps keeping Daisy at your side by using the treat. If at any time she loses interest in the treat, stop for that session. If she loses interest in the treat altogether, train her just using the leash-over-the-shoulder technique.

A word of caution: If Daisy is high in Prey *and* high in Defense (fight) drives, it is not a good idea to use treats as inducement; it will get her too excited about the treats and may cause her to assert herself against you. Put another way, she will start to take over and become pack leader, the very opposite of what training is supposed to accomplish. You can still use a treat as an occasional reward.

Incorporating Turns

Once Daisy has mastered the circle, you are ready to incorporate turns. As part of the Canine Good Citizen test, walking on a loose leash includes:
- changes of directions
- a Left Turn
- a Right Turn
- an About Turn (to the right)

Daisy will have to demonstrate that her attention is on you and that she responds to your movements and changes of pace.

For the Left Turn, you will need to teach Daisy to get out of your way so you don't trip on each other. Before you make the turn, draw back on the leash, then make the turn and let go of the leash again. If she is paying attention to you, she will quickly pick up your body cues in making the turn after several repetitions. Practice until you can make a Left Turn without having to draw back on the leash. For the Right and About Turns, encourage her to stay with you by saying her name in an excited tone of voice just before you make the turn.

When practicing turns, keep in mind that there should be no doubt that Daisy is attentive to you and responds to your changes of direction. If you make a Left Turn and crash into Daisy because she keeps going straight, or if you make an About or a Right Turn only to have both of you going in opposite directions, it is obvious that Daisy is not paying the slightest bit of attention to you.

During the test you are permitted to talk to Daisy and give extra commands, so you are allowed to say her name to get her attention fixed on you before you make a turn and to tell her "Sit" when you come to a Halt.

ALTERNATIVE ONE

If after several training sessions you find your dog ignores your tugs, or worse yet, drags you the length of a football field so that your arms are now two inches longer and you are wearing gloves, try using a training collar. We recommend a nylon snap-around collar that fits your dog exactly. Measure Daisy's neck with a measuring tape *slightly below the ears*. That measurement is the correct collar size for your dog. *A larger collar will be too loose.*

One complaint we frequently hear is that a correctly fitted collar is too tight and too difficult to get on. If your measurement was correct, the collar cannot be too tight. You also need to know that when you start to put the collar on, many dogs will flex their neck muscles, thereby increasing the circumference of the neck by as much as a half-inch. Naturally, the collar will seem too tight and difficult to put on. Don't worry, once your dog's neck muscles are relaxed the collar will fit perfectly.

The principle of the tug and the immediate letting go of the leash are the same. Using a correctly fitted training collar will give you a greater measure of control as you try to teach Daisy to walk on a loose leash.

Note: You are not allowed to use this collar when taking the Canine Good Citizen test—it is only a training aid. Once Daisy has learned to walk on a loose leash, you can go back to using a buckle collar.

ALTERNATIVE TWO

Still not getting anywhere? Then try a head halter. Your dog may need several practice sessions to get used to it, but once it is

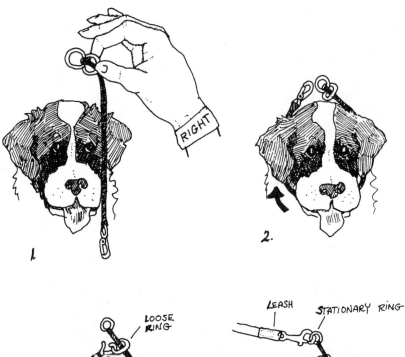

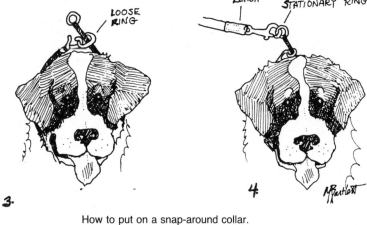

How to put on a snap-around collar.

accepted, she will readily respond to the training. The head halter is based on the principle that where the dog's head goes, the body has to follow. It is to be used only when walking or training your dog and *only* for control and guidance. *Never* tug on the halter! Once Daisy has the idea, try again with a regular collar.

> **Note:** You are not allowed to use a halter when taking the Canine Good Citizen test—it is only a training aid. It is a transitional tool, one that allows you to get a measure of control so that you can then train with a collar.

100

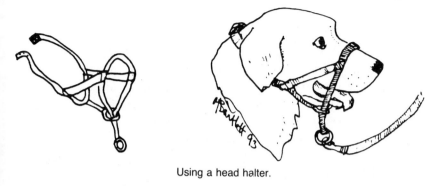

Using a head halter.

If your pet supply store does not carry these items, they can order them for you or advise you where to buy them.

THREE'S A CROWD

Once Daisy understands the basic principle of walking on a loose leash and stays with you during changes in direction, you are ready to introduce her to distractions. Remember, for the Canine Good Citizen test, Daisy is expected to walk close to at least three persons, demonstrating that she is conditioned to behave at all times and is under control in public places.

Start by introducing Daisy to the presence of other people gradually. For example, if you have practiced in your own backyard or an area free from distractions, seek out a location that has some distractions. The number of distractions in a given area often depends on the time of day. A school playground will be deserted at certain times, just as other public places have their ebb and flow of activity. Before you try Daisy during the height of an area's activity, practice with her during a lull. Make sure she is paying attention to you and responds to you. Should she become interested in another person and start straining at her leash, give her a tug on the leash to remind her to pay attention to you, and then praise her when she does what you want.

As she becomes accustomed to those surroundings, make it a little more difficult. Walk her past a stranger and watch her reaction. While she may show some interest in the stranger, she should pass by without showing shyness or resentment, and without straining at the leash. Ideally, she is paying attention to you. If not, remind her with a tug, followed by praise.

You will have to gauge how these distractions affect her and how much practice under those conditions Daisy requires. Some dogs couldn't care less about other people in their immediate vicinity, while others become highly distracted, even agitated, their responses dictated by the strength of their drives.

Much more distracting than people are dogs and especially loose dogs. You will find it difficult to practice with Daisy if another dog comes up to her for any reason, and you will have to seek a location where this is unlikely to happen.

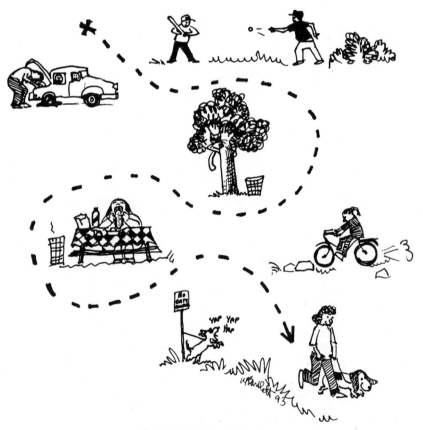

Practicing around distractions.

JUST WALKING

Having a dog know how to heel at your left side demonstrates control and is useful under circumstances where your dog needs to stay close to you and pay attention to you, such as around other people and dogs. Still, for many of us, the main reason we take our dogs for a walk is for daily exercise where it does not really matter what the dog does, so long as she does not pull. Usually the dog is somewhere ahead of us, checking out who has been there and just sort of following her nose.

For this type of a walk it makes little sense to have Daisy do a Heel since the main enjoyment for the dog is to use her nose and all you want from her is not to pull. Following is a simple, yet effective way to teach Daisy to remain within the length of your 6-foot leash *without pulling*.

Start to walk with ''Let's go,'' and as soon as Daisy gets to the end of the leash and starts to pull, stop and say ''Easy.'' Daisy's reaction will be to turn toward you and come back a few steps. Start walking again with ''Let's go,'' and when you begin to feel tension on the leash, stop with ''Easy.''

You may have to repeat this sequence a few times over the course of several sessions. If you do it consistently, Daisy will quickly learn that pulling causes you to stop, which in turn will cause her to stop pulling.

Like any other exercise you have taught Daisy, she will regress with time and you will periodically have to review the procedure.

TRAINING SCHEDULE

Week One

Walking

With your dog sitting at your left side, both of you facing in the same direction with the leash placed over your right shoulder, say ''Daisy, Heel,'' and start to walk at a brisk pace. Keep your hands *off* the leash. If your dog *starts* to leave your side, bring the dog back with a tug on the leash with either the left or both hands. Let go of the leash and verbally praise your dog. Practice five

The finished product.

sessions this week. Your **goal** is being able to walk for ten steps with your dog remaining at your left side without any tension on the leash. **Hint:** Walking will go a lot more smoothly if your dog is well exercised before you start to practice.

Halt

Every time you come to a Halt, have Daisy sit at your side by placing your right hand against the dog's chest and your left behind the stifles, folding her into a Sit with "Sit." As you come to a Halt, place your right knee on the ground and sit Daisy in line with your left leg. Every time you start to walk again, use the command "Daisy, Heel." Remember to *walk briskly*. Praise your dog when she stays with you *and* when she looks at you.

You can practice walking at the same session as the Sit, Down and Stand.

Week Two

Walking

Practice five sessions this week. Your goal is being able to walk for thirty steps with your dog remaining at your left side without any tension on the leash.

104

Halt

Each time you come to a Halt, pull up on the collar with your left hand with "Sit."

Week Three

Walking

Practice five sessions this week. Your goal is walking your dog in a large circle with Daisy remaining at your side without any tension on the leash.

Halt

Each time you do a Halt, pull up on the collar with your left hand *without saying anything*. If your dog responds, praise; if not, pull up on the collar with your left hand and say "Sit."

Week Four

Walking

Introduce changes of direction when walking. For the Left Turn, draw back on the leash before you make the turn, make the turn and let go of the leash again. For the Right and About Turns, encourage your dog to stay with you by saying her name in an excited tone of voice before you make the turn. Practice three each per session for five sessions this week. Your goal for this week is to be able to make turns while walking without having to help Daisy.

Halt

The goal for this exercise is to have Daisy do a Sit when you halt without any help from you, such as pulling up on the collar or having to say "Sit." Your stopping becomes her cue to do a Sit. Practice several times per session and be prepared to pull up on the collar in case she needs to be reminded that you want her to do a Sit when you halt. **Note:** Although the CGC does not require your dog to do a Sit when you halt, you may sit your dog when you do stop by using a command, such as ''Sit.'' We do not recommend that during the test you *physically* place your dog into a Sit or pull up on the leash. *The entire object of the test is to demonstrate that you are in control.*

Weeks Five Through Eight

See Chapter 8, Training with Distractions.

8

Training with Distractions

ONE OF THE MAIN GOALS of the Canine Good Citizen test is to demonstrate that the handler is in control of the dog under conditions the dog is likely to encounter on an almost daily basis, such as people and dogs engaged in a variety of activities. You will have to demonstrate that Max responds to the basic commands of Sit and Heel in real-life settings. As a catch-all, we call these conditions *distractions*, and six of the ten tests for the Canine Good Citizen involve the dog's reaction to a distraction.

Accepting a Friendly Stranger—requires the dog to allow a stranger to approach its owner. The evaluator walks up to the dog and owner and greets the owner in a friendly manner, ignoring the dog. They shake hands and exchange pleasantries, during which the dog must show no sign of resentment or shyness, and must not break position to try to go to the evaluator.

Sitting Politely for Petting—demonstrates that the dog will allow the approach of a stranger and permit petting. With the dog sitting at the owner's left side throughout the test, the evaluator approaches to pet the dog on the head and body only. The dog must

Accepting a friendly stranger.   *Photo by Jack Volhard*

not show shyness or resentment, and the evaluator then circles the dog and owner.

Appearance and Grooming—requires that the dog can be groomed and examined by a stranger, such as a veterinarian. The evaluator inspects the dog to determine if it is clean and groomed. The dog must appear to be in a healthy condition, including being the proper weight.

This particular test demonstrates the owner's care, concern and responsibility for the dog. The evaluator then easily combs or brushes the dog to show the dog's willingness to be groomed and permit someone other than its owner to do so. The evaluator also lightly and in a natural manner examines the ears and gently picks up each front foot. For some reason many dogs have difficulty with this exercise and you may have to spend a little extra time getting Max used to having his feet handled.

Walking Through a Crowd—requires the dog and owner to walk around and close to several persons—at least three, one of whom may have a dog—demonstrating that the dog is conditioned to behave at all times and is under control in public places. The dog may show some interest in the strangers, but should continue to walk with the owner without evidence of exuberance, shyness or resentment. The dog should not be straining at the leash.

Praise/Interaction—requires a demonstration of your ability to calm your dog after play.

Reaction to Another Dog—requires a demonstration of proper behavior when in the presence of other dogs. Two handlers and their dogs approach each other from a distance of about 10 yards, stop, shake hands and exchange pleasantries, and continue on about 5 yards. This is another potentially difficult exercise—many dogs want to say "hello" to the other dog, which is not permitted. Short of practicing with other dogs, a *solid* Sit-Stay should see you through this exercise successfully.

Reaction to Distraction—requires a demonstration of the dog's confidence when faced with distracting situations, which can be any two of the following, usually one auditory and one visual:

- a person using crutches, a wheelchair or a walker
- sudden closing or opening of a door
- dropping a large book, no closer than 10 feet behind the dog
- a jogger running in front of the dog
- good-natured pushing and shoving or animated excited talk and back-slapping by persons, with the dog and handler passing within 10 feet
- a person pushing a cart approaching from the front or rear, passing within 10 feet
- a person on a bicycle approaching from the front or rear, passing about 6 feet to the side of the dog
- knocking over a chair, no closer than 6 feet from the dog

The dog may express natural interest and curiosity or may startle but should not panic, try to run away, show aggressiveness or bark.

Sitting politely for petting.   *Photo by Jack Volhard*

Except for the ***Sitting Politely for Petting***, the regulations do not specify the dog's position for these tests. Even so, we suggest that you use the Sit-Stay as the basic position for the dog. It is practical, useful, easy to teach and gives the dog a specific task on which to focus.

SELF-GENERATED DISTRACTIONS

Introduce Max to the concept of distraction training with the Sit-Stay. Start with your dog sitting at your left side. Say and use a signal to "Stay," and step 3 feet in front of Max. Now take a step to your right. If Max moves or thinks about moving, reinforce the Stay by slapping the leash with your right hand as you *repeat* "Stay." Step back to the middle, then to the left, back to the middle, backward and forward. The idea is to teach Max not to move even when tempted and to hold position in the face of distractions. Any time you think Max may move, reinforce the Stay. After one complete set of stepping to the right, middle, etc., return to your dog's side, pause, praise and release. Repeat the procedure except jump to the right, middle, etc.

Then do a Sit-Stay from in front while clapping your hands, first quietly, and then more enthusiastically. As Max becomes more and more steady, add clapping and cheering.

TRAINING WITH A HELPER

Now that Max is reliable with self-generated distractions, you are ready to introduce him to other distractions. We suggest that you start by teaching him the Sit for examination and then build from there. You will need a helper for these exercises.

With Max sitting at your left side, both of you facing the same direction, begin as you did for the Sit-Stay. Put the leash, neatly folded, into your left hand with the part that goes to the dog coming out at the bottom of your hand and the ring of the collar on top of the dog's neck. Say and/or use the signal "Stay" and have your helper approach Max from 6 feet at a 45 degree angle to your left. Have the helper approach in a friendly and nonthreatening manner, without hovering over the dog. Have the helper present Max the palm of a hand and continue to walk by. If Max stays, praise and release. If Max wants to get up, check straight up with your left hand with "Stay" and try again.

Your dog's score in Defense (fight) or (flight) drive will determine the response to a helper. For example, if the helper is a stranger and Max is high in Defense (fight), he may show signs of aggression toward the helper. On the other hand, if low in Defense (fight) and high in Defense (flight), Max may try to hide behind you when the helper approaches or show signs of shyness. Since the Sit for Examination is the cornerstone for all the distraction tests, you need to condition Max to perform this exercise correctly before you continue.

Training with a helper.   *Photo by Jack Volhard*

The helper can make the difference in how Max is conditioned. Max's response determines how close he or she gets in the beginning. If the dog becomes apprehensive about the helper's approach, we suggest that the person walk past the dog at a distance of 2 feet without making eye contact with or even looking at the dog. As the dog gets used to that maneuver, have the helper offer a treat, placed on the open palm to the dog, as he or she walks by, still without making eye contact with the dog. It does not matter whether the dog takes the treat or not—it's the gesture that counts.

When the dog accepts that, have the helper first offer a treat and then pet the dog on the head, still without making eye contact, as he or she continues on past the dog. After that, the helper can attempt to look at the dog as he or she touches the dog and goes past. For this particular dog, it is the eye contact in connection with the examination that is the hard part of the exercise, and it may require several sessions before the dog is steady.

The ultimate aim of this exercise is that the dog allow the approach of a stranger who will then also pet the dog. For the majority of dogs, this is not a particularly difficult exercise, but it does require a little practice.

Appearance and Grooming is a similar test and one that can be introduced as soon as your dog accepts petting by a stranger. Have your helper lightly comb or brush Max with you at your dog's side or directly in front. Remember to have your helper lightly examine the ears and pick up each front foot. If your dog finds this difficult, have the helper give the dog a treat as he or she touches a foot. Condition the dog with praise and treats to accept having the feet handled.

Since your dog's profile determines how he reacts to a particular distraction, you need to expose Max to the different distractions to see how he deals with them. Some dogs take it all in stride and others require several exposures to become accustomed to the distraction. The best foundation is a solid Sit-Stay.

SUPERVISED ISOLATION

While not specifically dealing with distractions, this test fits into this general category. It shows that the dog can be left alone, which demonstrates training and good manners. Actually, Max is not really left alone, it is just that you are out of sight. At the very least, an evaluator is present to watch him, and in some cases, other dogs are in the immediate vicinity who are also doing this test. The dog should not bark, whine, howl or pace unnecessarily or register anything other than mild agitation or nervousness.

As part of the test, the owner fastens the dog to a 6-foot line and goes out of sight of the dog for three minutes. You can leave Max in either the Sit or the Down position. It is not necessary for the dog to hold that position until you return, only that he does not vocalize or pace unnecessarily. Still, by having Max focus on staying in place, you reduce the likelihood that he will bark or howl, or become overly agitated. It can be done as a simple Down-Stay exercise with the owner out of sight, which is what we recommend, with the dog attached to the line for reasons of safety.

The first time we became aware of how useful this test really

Supervised isolation.

Photo by Jack Volhard

is, was during a visit to Frankfurt, Germany. In Germany, dogs are allowed almost everywhere—even restaurants. Then we noticed that many food stores, where dogs are not allowed, had a hook outside at dog level to which a customer could attach the pet while shopping inside. This was sort of like a hitching post for dogs.

PRAISE/INTERACTION

For this test you need to demonstrate that you can control your dog after a certain amount of "play." Only you know how excited you can get your dog and still retain your control. If Max is high in Prey drive behaviors, it is probably not a good idea to use a toy or a ball for this test because you may have a hard time getting him under control again.

In case of doubt, limit yourself to praising and getting your dog's tail to wag. For the test it is not necessary that he actually play; he only needs to be passively agreeable to praise.

NEW LOCATIONS

To be successful in your efforts toward a Canine Good Citizen certificate, you will need to seek out new and different locations in which to train. Max may be the perfect student at home and in familiar surroundings, but in strange places and with new distractions he will give the appearance of abject stupidity and stubbornness. Some owners actually think that Max lies awake at night thinking of ways to be embarrassing in public. Fortunately, this is not the case—Max simply has not been sufficiently conditioned to respond under all circumstances.

Keep this rule in mind: One training session in a new location is three to five times as valuable as a training session at home.

TRAINING SCHEDULE

Week Five

Sit

Have your dog sit at your left side, on leash. Signal and say "Stay" and go 3 feet in front. Make sure the dog is paying attention to you. Take a step to the right and if your dog *looks* as though he wants to move, reinforce the Stay. Take a step to the right, middle, left, middle, backward and forward. Anytime Max tries to move, reinforce the Stay. When Max is steady with you stepping to the right, etc., repeat by *jumping* to the right, etc. Your goal is for Max to remain rooted to the spot during these maneuvers without you having to reinforce the Stay by the end of the training week.

Down

Practice the same sequence as above for the Down-Stay. Remember to use random rewards when Max lies down on command and without you having to touch the collar.

Stand

Stand your dog, signal and say "Stay" and step directly in front. Count to ten, step back, praise, pause and release. If your dog moves, reposition him. Your goal for the training week is being able to stand in front for one minute without Max moving.

Walking

Practice in an area where you will encounter some distractions while walking. Should your dog become distracted, say his name to get the attention back on you, then enthusiastically praise or reward with a treat. If you still cannot get attention when you say your dog's name, reinforce the Heel command with a check and then praise when the dog looks at you.

Week Six

Sit

Review what you practiced last week. When your dog is steady, add clapping as a form of distraction, first quietly and then more loudly. When Max is steady with your clapping, you can add cheering.

Introduce your dog to the **Sitting Politely for Petting**. First have your helper walk close by and if your dog stays, have the helper touch the dog on top of the head, and then run his or her hand down your dog's back.

Three times this week, leave your dog on a 20-foot line on a Sit-Stay and go 10 feet in front with the line in hand. Count to ten and return. If your dog moves, put him back and repeat the exercise. Your goal at the end of the training week is for Max to stay in place until you return.

Down

Practice the same sequence as above for the Down-Stay. Introduce your dog to the **Supervised Isolation** test. Attach a 6-foot line to the dog and attach the line to something solid. Go out of your dog's sight for ten seconds. Return and praise enthusiastically. Your goal by the end of the training week is to leave Max for one minute.

We recommend that you practice this exercise once per training session in ten-second increments. In the beginning, while Max is learning to cope with this exercise, you don't want to stay away too long.

Stand

This week introduce self-generated distractions—step to the right, the middle, the left, backward, forward—with you 3 feet in front. If Max moves, reposition him.

Walking

This week make it a little more difficult by walking Max past a stranger. If he is distracted, reinforce attention on you with a check. Praise and reward with a treat when Max looks at you. If you can't practice in an area with strangers, solicit a friend to act the part of the stranger.

Use your friend to practice the ***Accepting a Friendly Stranger*** test. With Max sitting at your left side, say "Stay." Have your helper approach you in a friendly manner, shake hands and exchange pleasantries. If Max tries to move or go to your helper, reinforce the Stay. Practice three times in a row. Depending on Max's response, you may have to practice this exercise several times this week. Your goal is for Max to remain sitting at your side during the ***Accepting a Friendly Stranger*** test.

Note: Your helper can be a member of the family as long as you keep in mind that Max will be more tempted to go to him or her than if the helper were a complete stranger. In a sense, the test is made more difficult by using a family member. On the other hand, if Max has a tendency to be fearful of strangers, a family member makes the test easier, and you will need to practice with a stranger or someone Max does not know well.

Week Seven

Sit

Review the Sit-Stay from 3 feet in front. Practice the Sit for petting with a helper and have the helper lightly examine your dog's ears, pick up *each* front foot and lightly comb or brush your dog.

117

Three times this week, put your dog on a 20-foot line, leave your dog on a Sit-Stay and with the line in hand walk forward the length of the line, count to ten and return. If Max moves, put him back and repeat the exercise. Your goal at the end of the training week is for Max to stay in place until you return.

Down

Be sure your dog responds to the Down command without you having to touch or *reach* for the collar. Three times this week, leave your dog on a Down-Stay and go 20 feet in front, count to ten and return. If Max moves, put him back and repeat the exercise. Practice **Supervised Isolation**. Your goal by the end of the training week is to leave Max for three minutes.

Stand

From 3 feet in front, *jump* to the right, etc. If Max moves, reposition him.

Walking

Practice for no more than three minutes walking in an area with distractions. If your dog is distracted, reinforce attention on you with a check. Praise and reward with a treat when the dog looks at you. If Max is paying attention to you, he will not be too concerned about passing close by other people. Once this week practice the **Accepting a Stranger** test.

Week Eight

Sit

Review those parts of the exercise that seem difficult for your dog or that have not been mastered. For the **Sitting Politely for Petting**, have your helper examine the dog by lightly combing or brushing Max, examining the ears and picking up *each* front foot.

Down

Practice **Supervised Isolation**. Your goal by the end of the training week is to leave Max for six minutes.

Stand

Practice a Stand-Stay with you standing 6 feet in front for thirty seconds.

Walking

Practice for no more than three minutes walking around distractions and keeping Max's attention on you. Once this week practice the **Accepting a Stranger** test.

You only have a dog **if** your dog comes when called!

9

Coming When Called

DEMONSTRATING that your dog will come when called is *not* a requirement for the Canine Good Citizen test. Even so, we strongly urge you to teach the Come command to your dog. One of the greatest joys of owning a dog is to eventually be able to go for a walk in a park or the woods and let your dog run, knowing she will come when called. A dog that does not come when called is a prisoner of the leash and, if loose, a danger to itself and others.

If your dog does not come when called, you don't have a dog!

Following are five rules to help you teach this command to Daisy:

RULE ONE

Exercise, exercise, exercise.

Many dogs do not come when called because they do not get enough physical exercise. When they do get the chance, they run off and make the most of it by staying out for hours at a time. Every morning your dog wakes up with X amount of energy or need to exercise. If that energy is not used up, it will transform itself into other behaviors, the most common of which are barking, chewing, digging, self-mutilation and, of course, running away or not coming when called.

Consider what your dog was bred to do and that will tell you how much exercise is needed. We doubt that a few turns around the backyard will suffice for Daisy. You will need to participate. Think of it this way, taking the dog for a daily walk or jog is as good for you as it is for your dog!

RULE TWO

Whenever your dog comes to you, *be nice* to her.

One of the quickest ways to teach your dog *not* to come to you is to call Daisy to you, and when she comes, punish her or do something *she* perceives as unpleasant. Many dogs consider being given a bath or a pill unpleasant. When Daisy needs either one, go and get her *instead of* calling her to you.

Another example of teaching your dog not to come is to take her for a run in the park and call her to you when it's time to go home. Repeating this sequence several times teaches the dog the party is over! Soon, Daisy may become reluctant to return to you when called because she is not ready to end the fun.

You can prevent this kind of unintentional training by calling Daisy to you several times during the outing, sometimes giving her a treat, sometimes just a pat on the head, and then letting her romp again.

RULE THREE

Teach Daisy to come when called as soon as you bring her home, no matter how young she is.

Ideally, you acquired Daisy as a puppy and that is the best time to teach her to come when called. Start right away. But remember, sometime between the fourth and eighth months of age, your puppy will begin to realize there is a big, wide world out there. (See Chapter 3, What Happens When?)

While she is going through this stage, it is best to keep Daisy on leash so that she does not learn to ignore you when you call.

RULE FOUR

When in doubt, keep your dog on leash.

Learn to anticipate when your dog is likely *not to come*. You may be tempting fate trying to call once Daisy has spotted a cat, another dog or a jogger. Of course, there will be times when you goof and let her go just as another dog appears out of nowhere.

Resist the urge to make a complete fool of yourself by bellowing "Come" a million times. The more often you holler "Come," the quicker she learns to ignore you when off leash. Instead, patiently go to your dog and put Daisy on leash. Do not get angry once you have caught her or you will make her afraid of you. She will then run away when you try to catch her the next time.

RULE FIVE

Make sure your dog always comes to you and lets you touch the collar *before* you reward with a treat or praise.

Make sure dog lets you touch the collar *before* you reward her.

Touching the collar prevents the dog from developing the annoying habit of playing "catch," which means coming toward you and then dancing around you, just out of reach.

THE GAME OF COMING WHEN CALLED

Needed: two people, one hungry dog, one 6-foot leash and plenty of small treats.

Step One:

Inside the house, with your dog on a 6-foot leash, you and your partner sit on the floor, 6 feet apart, facing each other. Your partner gently hangs on to the dog, you hold the end of the leash. Call your dog by saying "Daisy, Come," and use the leash to guide her to you. Grasp the collar *under* her chin, palm up, give a treat, pet and praise enthusiastically.

Now you hold Daisy and pass the leash to your partner, who says "Daisy, Come," guides the dog in, grasps the collar, gives a treat and praises the dog.

Goal: Repeat until your dog responds voluntarily to being called and no longer needs to be guided in with the leash.

Step Two:

Repeat Step One with your dog off leash.

Goal: Gradually increase distance between you and your partner to 12 feet.

Step Three:

Have your partner hold your dog (off leash) while you hide from Daisy (go into another room), then call your dog. When she finds you, grasp the collar, give a treat and praise. If she can't find you, go to her, take the collar and bring her to the spot where you called. Reward and praise. Now have your partner hide and then call the dog.

Goal: Repeat until the dog doesn't hesitate in finding you or your partner in any room of the house.

124

The Recall Game.

GOING OUTSIDE

Take your dog outside to a confined area, such as a fenced yard, tennis court, park or school yard and repeat steps one, two and three.

You are now ready to practice by yourself. Let Daisy loose in a confined area and ignore her. When she is *not* paying any attention to you, call. When she gets to you, give a treat and make a big fuss. If she does not come, go to her, take the collar and bring her to the spot where you called. Then reward and praise her.

Repeat until Daisy comes to you *every* time you call.

Once your dog is trained, you don't have to reward with a treat every time, but do so frequently.

ADDING DISTRACTIONS

Some dogs will need to be trained to come in the face of distractions such as other dogs, children, joggers, food or friendly strangers. Think about the most irresistible situations for your dog and then practice under those circumstances.

On-Leash Distractions

Step One: Put a 12-foot leash on Daisy (this can be two 6-foot leashes tied together) and take her to an area where you are likely

Recall *on* leash with distractions.

to encounter her favorite distraction (jogger, bicycle, other dog, whatever). Once she gets distracted, let her become thoroughly engrossed, either by watching or straining at the leash, and give the command "Daisy, Come." More than likely, she will ignore you. Give a firm tug on the leash and guide her back to you. Praise and pet her enthusiastically.

Goal: Repeat three times per session until the dog turns and comes to you *immediately* when you call.

Note: Some dogs quickly learn to avoid the distraction by staying close to you, which is fine. Tell Daisy what a clever girl she is and then try with a different distraction at another time.

126

Recall *off* leash with distractions.

Step Two: Repeat Step One in different locations with as many different distractions as you can find. Try it with someone offering your dog a tidbit as a distraction (the person is *not* to let the dog have the treat), someone petting the dog and anything else that may distract her. Use your imagination.

   Goal: A dog that comes immediately when called, even when distracted.

Off-Leash Distractions

How you approach this part of the training will depend on your individual circumstances. Here is an example:

Take your dog to an area where you are not likely to encounter distractions in the form of other dogs or people. Remove the leash and let Daisy become involved in a smell in the grass or a tree. Keep the distance between you and her about 10 feet. Call her. If you get the desired response, praise enthusiastically. If not, avoid the temptation to call again. Don't worry; she heard you, but chose to ignore you. Instead, slowly walk up behind her, grasp the collar under the chin, palm up, and trot backward to the spot from where you called. Then praise. Repeat until she comes the *first* time you call.

Once Daisy is reliable at this point, try an area with other distractions. If she does not respond, practice for the correct response with the 12-foot leash before you try it again off leash.

Can you now trust Daisy to come in an unconfined area? That will depend on how well you have done your homework and what your dog may encounter in the "real" world. Understanding your dog and what things interest her will help you know when she is not likely to respond to being called.

When in doubt, keep your dog on leash.

Let common sense be your guide. For example, when you are traveling and have to let your dog out at a busy interstate rest stop, it would be foolhardy to do so off leash. Remember Rule Four: When in doubt, keep her on leash.

SUMMARY

1) If your dog does not come when called, you don't have a dog.
2) Whenever your dog comes to you, be nice and reward that response.
3) When in doubt, keep your dog on leash.
4) Always grasp the collar under the chin, palm up, after your dog has come to you and before you give a reward.
5) Teach your dog to come when called *now*.
6) "Come" is the most important command you can teach your dog.

Do give your dog a bath

10

Taking the Test

ORGANIZATIONS OFFERING the Canine Good Citizen test have considerable leeway in making up the order in which to give the tests. The most common order is:

1. Accepting a Friendly Stranger
2. Sitting Politely for Petting
3. Appearance and Grooming
4. Out for a Walk (walk on a loose leash)
5. Walking Through a Crowd
6. Sit and Down on Command/Staying in Place
7. Praise/Interaction
8. Reaction to Another Dog
9. Reaction to Distractions
10. Supervised Isolation

The Supervised Isolation test may take place in the presence of other dogs that are also doing this test.

Usually three evaluators conduct the test. The first evaluator conducts tests one through three, the second one tests four through nine and the third one test ten. The test is evaluated on a pass/fail basis, and in order to qualify for a Canine Good Citizen certificate, the dog must pass each of the ten tests.

An automatic failure results when a dog eliminates during testing, except during test ten, *provided* it is held outdoors. *Handlers are also not permitted to give their dogs food when the dog is being tested.*

Any dog that growls, snaps, bites, attacks or attempts to attack a person or another dog is *not* a good citizen and must be dismissed from the test.

To participate in a Canine Good Citizen test you need to bring and *present*, at the time of the test, a current rabies certificate and any other state or locally required inoculations and licenses.

Following are a few dos and don'ts that will help you in preparing for and participating in the Canine Good Citizen test.

DOS

Do practice the entire test with a helper and friends before you actually enter a test. This is more for your benefit than Max's. As you become familiar with the test, you will lose some of your nervousness. It will also identify Max's weak areas and give you additional time to work on them.

Do give your dog a bath and thoroughly groom him before the test.

Do use the correct equipment for the test—a well-fitting buckle or slip collar of either leather, fabric or chain, and a leather or fabric leash.

Do exercise your dog before you take the test. Should any dog eliminate at any time during testing, that dog must be marked failed.

Do warm up your dog before taking the test so that both of you are as relaxed as possible under the circumstances.

Do use a second command for any exercise if necessary.

Do talk to your dog during an exercise to keep attention on you if necessary.

132

Don't do anything you don't ordinarily do.

Do ask the evaluator if you don't understand a procedure or an instruction.

Do maintain a *loose* leash throughout the *entire* test, even between exercises, to the extent possible. While an occasional tightening of the leash is generally not considered a failure, it does become a judgment call for the evaluator in assessing your control over your dog. It is best not to put yourself or the evaluator in that position.

Do understand that *your* attitude and state of mind are the most important influence on the outcome of the test. If you are excessively nervous, your dog will become nervous, too. Handlers under stress at times will do things they would never dream of doing any other time. If this happens, it will be confusing to the point where the dog might fail. Maintain a positive outlook and rely on your training.

Do conduct yourself in a sportsmanlike manner at all times.

DON'TS

Don't lose your temper or attitude if your dog should fail an exercise. If you berate your dog you will sour him or her on the entire experience. You will feel a certain amount of disappointment and perhaps frustration, but those feelings, too, you need to control. The more you work as a team, the more your dog can sense your feelings, but will associate them with the circumstances and the failure of an exercise.

Ideally, there should be no change in your attitude toward your dog after failing an exercise, so that the dog is completely unaware that something went wrong. Your remedy is *not* to make the dog feel stupid or anxious, but to review your training, work on the difficult exercise and try again. If your dog's confidence is undermined, training will take longer and become a less rewarding experience than if you realize that your job is to help your dog at every step of the way by support and encouragement.

Don't do anything you don't ordinarily do—it is amazing how people do things during the test they would ordinarily never dream of doing. You will hopelessly confuse your dog.

Keep in mind the purpose of the Canine Good Citizen and become an ambassador of goodwill and good manners for all dogs. Good luck!

11

Summary of Exercises

BASIC CONTROL

Week One

Thirty-minute Down with you next to your dog. Use the command Down as you place and every time you place Daisy into the Down position. Release with "OK" after thirty minutes, even if your dog has fallen asleep. Practice three times a week, more if your dog continually tries to get up.

Week Two

Practice the *thirty-minute Down* and the *ten-minute Sit* on alternate days with you sitting in a chair next to your dog. If Daisy gets up or tries to move out of position, put her back.

Week Three

Practice the *thirty-minute Down* and the *ten-minute Sit* on alternate days with you sitting across the room from your dog. If Daisy gets up or tries to move out of position, put her back.

Week Four

Practice the *thirty-minute Down* and the *ten-minute sit* on alternate days with you moving about, but not leaving the room. If Daisy gets up or tries to move out of position, put her back.

Note: *This basic control regimen is an absolute must before you attempt any further training with Daisy.* It sets the stage for a harmonious training experience and one where Daisy accepts you as her pack leader.

RESPONSE TO COMMANDS

Week One

Sit

Five times per session sit your dog with "Sit," using a treat or placing Daisy into a Sit. Remember to verbally praise her enthusiastically when she responds. *Do not use your hands to pet Daisy as a form of praise.* Practice five days a week together with the Down.

Down

Five times per session down your dog with "Down," using a treat and two fingers of the left hand through the collar or placing Daisy into the Down. Praise when she responds.

Stand

Stand your dog—thumb through collar under the chin, palm against chest, backward pressure on stifles with left hand—with "Stand." Daisy's front feet are supposed to remain in place as she brings her rear up from the sitting position. Practice having her stand still for one minute, readjusting her if necessary. After one minute give lots of praise followed by a release. Remember that praise is not an invitation to move—it only means you are doing the right thing, keep it up, mommy loves you, etc.

Walking

Practice with the leash over the right shoulder, in a large counterclockwise circle. Say "Daisy, Heel," and start to walk at a brisk pace. If necessary, use the left or both hands to bring Daisy back to your left side with a check and let go of the leash again. Keep your hands off the leash unless you have to bring Daisy back to the Heel position. Praise her enthusiastically when she stays with you and anytime she looks at you.

Every time you come to a Halt, say "Sit" and place Daisy into a Sit by putting your right hand against her chest and placing her into a Sit with the left. As you come to a Halt, place your right knee on the ground and sit Daisy in line with your left leg. **Goal:** Practice until you can walk for ten steps with your dog remaining at your side and without having to touch the leash.

Week Two

Sit

Practice having your dog sit with two fingers of your left hand in the collar at the top of her neck. Say "Sit" and if Daisy sits, give her a treat. If she doesn't, pull up on the collar to make her do a Sit, then give her a treat and praise her. Count to ten and release. Practice five times per session for five days.

Stay

Leash neatly folded into your left hand, rings of the collar on top of the dog's neck, apply slight upward tension on the collar, take a step to the right, count to ten, step back, release tension and praise. Repeat by standing directly in front of your dog. If she moves, put her back. **Goal:** thirty seconds in front of Daisy, without her moving after five sessions. *Hint:* If you stand still without fidgeting, your dog will stay.

Down

With two fingers of your left hand through the collar at the side of Daisy's neck, apply downward pressure on the collar and say "Down." Praise and give her a treat when she lies down, count to ten and release. Practice five times per session, five days a week.

Stand

Stand your dog—remember, the front feet should not move—and remove your left hand from the stifles. Practice keeping Daisy standing still for one minute once a session. If she moves, readjust her. After one minute praise, count to five and release.

Walking

Your goal for this week is to be able to walk Daisy for thirty steps without having to touch the leash. Practice five sessions a week. Each time you come to a Halt, pull straight up on the collar with your left hand and say "Sit." *Praise* Daisy when she does it correctly.

Week Three

Sit

This week's goal is for Daisy to respond to the Sit command without you having to touch or reach for her collar. Give her a treat for every correct response. Practice five times per session for five days.

Hint: Some dogs get bored quickly after they have responded correctly to a command and you may find that Daisy is a more motivated student if you don't do five repetitions in a row and do another exercise in between.

Stay

With Daisy sitting at your left side, rings of the collar under her chin, neatly fold the leash into your left hand, signal and say "Stay" and go 3 feet in front. Count to ten, return, praise, pause and release. If necessary, slap the leash with your right hand (reinforce) or put her back. Learn to reinforce the Stay while Daisy is *thinking* about moving. **Goal:** a one minute Sit-Stay at the end of the training week.

138

Down

This week's goal is for Daisy to lie down on command without you having to touch the collar. For every correct response, praise her and give a treat. Practice five times per session (not all at once) for five days.

Stand

Stand your dog and take both hands off. Be prepared to steady Daisy with your right hand against her chest, and if she moves, readjust her. Practice having Daisy do a Stand for one minute once a session.

Walking

This week's goal is to be able to walk Daisy once around in a large circle without having to touch the leash. Practice five sessions a week. Each time you do a Halt, pull up on the collar with your left hand *without* saying anything. If Daisy sits, praise enthusiastically; if she does not, take a step forward, repeat with "Sit," then praise.

Week Four

Sit

Begin to reward correct responses—Daisy does a Sit on command without you having to touch or reach for the collar—on *a random basis*.

Stay

Practice from 6 feet in front, on leash. For the first session, count to ten, return, pause, praise, and release. **Goal:** Gradually increase the time to one minute over the course of five training sessions.

Down

Begin to reward correct responses—Daisy does a Down on command without you having to touch or reach for the collar—on a *random* basis.

Stand

Practice having Daisy do a Stand for one minute once a session.

Walking

Introduce changes of direction. Draw back on the leash for the Left Turn, and encourage Daisy to stay with you on the Right and About Turns. Your goal for the week is to have Daisy stay with you during turns without any help from you. When you do a Halt, give Daisy a chance to do a Sit on her own, and only pull up on the collar when she does not Sit when you stop.

Sitting Politely for Petting test—two or three times this week practice this test with your helper. With Daisy at your left side, tell her to Stay. Have your helper approach in a friendly manner, and pet her on the head and body. Practice three times in a row.

Week Five

Sit

Continue to practice the ''Sit'' command using random rewards.

Stay

Practice from 3 feet in front, on leash, with self-generated distractions (first step to right, middle, left, middle, backward and forward, then repeat by jumping to the right, etc.). If necessary, reinforce the Stay command. **Goal:** for Daisy to remain rooted to the spot without you having to reinforce.

Down

Continue to use random rewards when Daisy responds to the ''Down'' command. Practice the same sequences for the Down-Stay as you do for the Sit-Stay.

Stand

Stand Daisy and step directly in front of her, count to ten, step back, praise, pause and release. **Goal:** You should be able to stand in front of Daisy for one minute without having to reposition her.

Walking

Practice in an area with some distractions and concentrate on keeping Daisy's attention on you for short periods of time before releasing her. Gradually build up the length of time you expect Daisy to pay attention to you between releases. **Goal:** Keep Daisy's attention for thirty seconds without having to reinforce.

Sitting Politely for Petting test—review if Daisy has difficulty with this test.

Week Six

Sit

Review what you practiced last week; first add clapping and then cheering. Three times this week put your dog on a 20-foot line, leave her on a Sit-Stay and go 10 feet in front, count to ten and return. If your dog moves, put her back.

Down

Practice the same sequences for the Down-Stay. *Supervised Isolation* test—introduce Daisy to this test. The first time you do this, go out of her sight for only fifteen seconds before you return to her. Work up to being able to leave her out of sight for one minute by the end of the training week.

Stand

Introduce self-generated distractions as you did for Week Five of the Sit-Stay. Introduce Daisy to the *Appearance and Grooming* test—with you at her side, have your helper lightly comb or brush Daisy. Practice three times a week.

Walking

Walk Daisy past a stranger. If necessary, reinforce attention on you. Introduce Daisy to the ***Accepting a Friendly Stranger*** test—with Daisy sitting at your left side, tell her "Stay." Have your helper approach in a friendly manner, shake hands and exchange pleasantries. Concentrate on having Daisy do a Sit at your left side and use the Stay command before you shake hands with your helper. If Daisy tries to move, reinforce the Stay.

Sitting Politely for Petting test—review.

Week Seven

Sit

Review what you practiced last week. Three times this week put your dog on a 20-foot line, leave her on a Sit-Stay and go 20 feet in front, count to ten 10 and return. If she moves, put her back.

Down

Review what you practiced last week. Work up to being able to leave her out of sight for three minutes by the end of the training week.

Stand

Introduce self-generated distractions as you did for Week Five of the Sit-Stay. Practice the ***Appearance and Grooming*** test three times. With you at her side, have your helper lightly comb or brush Daisy, and lightly examine the ears.

Walking

Try to find an area that has different distractions and one where you can walk Daisy close to more than one stranger. If necessary, reinforce attention on you. Review the ***Accepting a Friendly Stranger*** test. You will also have to find someone with a friendly, under-control dog to practice the ***Reaction to Another Dog*** test. View it as another Sit-Stay exercise.

Week Eight

Sit

Review what you practiced last week. Three times this week put your dog on a 20-foot line, leave her on a Sit-Stay and go 20 feet in front, count to ten and return. If she moves, put her back.

Down

Review what you practiced last week. ***Supervised Isolation*** test—go out of her sight for one minute before you return to her. Work up to being able to leave her out of sight for six minutes by the end of the training week.

Stand

Review with distractions. Three times practice the ***Appearance and Grooming*** test. With you at her side, have your helper lightly comb or brush Daisy, lightly examine her ears and lightly pick up each front foot.

Walking

Review with distractions. If necessary, reinforce attention on you.

Glossary

---

agent - *see* professional handler.

AKC - American Kennel Club. Keeps records of purebred dogs; regulates and oversees dog shows and performance events as well as purebred dog registrations.

automatic failure - in the Canine Good Citizen test, for dogs that eliminate, and for handlers who give food during the test.

Benched show - a dog show at which dogs are required to be displayed on ''benches'' during certain hours except when in the ring for judging.

Best in Show (BIS) - the dog judged best of all dogs of all breeds at a particular show.

Brace - two dogs of the same breed with identical ownership exhibited at the same time in either conformation or Obedience.

CD - Companion Dog. An Obedience title awarded by the AKC for dogs that have qualified in Novice classes at three different shows under three different judges. The exercises are Heel on Leash and Figure Eight, Stand for Examination, Heel Free, Recall, one-minute Sit and three-minute Down.

CDX - Companion Dog Excellent. An Obedience title awarded by the AKC for dogs that have qualified in three Open classes. Dogs must have earned a CD to enter the Open class. The exercises are Heel Free and Figure Eight, Drop on Recall, Retrieve on the Flat, Retrieve over High Jump, Broad Jump, three-minute Sit and five-minute Down with handler out of sight.

Ch. - Champion. An AKC conformation title.

check - a quick tug on the collar with an *immediate* release.

conformation - a dog's form, structure and temperament.

conformation show - an exhibition to determine how well a dog conforms to the Standard for a given breed. Dogs are exhibited in conformation to become champions.

dismissal - from the Canine Good Citizen test for growling, snapping, biting, attacks or attempted attacks on a person or another dog.

disqualification - a condition making a dog ineligible for exhibition at a dog show.

dog show - catchall for conformation shows and Obedience Trials.

Dog World Award of Canine Distinction - a performance award by *Dog World* magazine for particular conformation or Obedience accomplishments.

Draft Dog (DD) - a drafting title awarded by the Newfoundland Club of America.

drives - traits our dogs have inherited from their ancestors.

extrinsic - not from within; not inherent.

FCh. - Field Champion.

Field Trial - a competition for hunting dogs that are judged on their ability to retrieve game and follow direction.

"Gazette" - *see* Pure-Bred Dogs, The American Kennel Gazette.

handler - the person handling the dog, usually the owner. The terms "handler," "owner" or "trainer" are often used synonymously.

Heel position - with handler and dog facing in the same direction and the dog being as close to the handler as practical, the area from the dog's head to the shoulder is in line with the handler's left hip.

Highest Scoring Dog in Trial (HIT) - from either the Novice, Open or Utility class, the dog with the highest score of all the dogs competing in regular class Obedience at a given show.

intrinsic - from within; no outside influence.

Landseer - white-and-black Newfoundland dog.

latent learning - the process of absorbing what is being taught by taking a break.

leg - a qualifying score toward an Obedience title.

match show - a practice show at which no championship points or qualifying scores are awarded.

negative stress - manifests itself in the dog becoming lethargic and tired.

Novice class - *see* **CD**.

NQ - a nonqualifying performance in an Obedience class.

Obedience title - CD, CDX, UD, OTCh., TD and TDX.

Obedience Trial - dogs compete for Obedience titles.

Open class - *see* **CDX**.

OTCh. - Obedience Trial Champion. An Obedience title awarded by the AKC for dogs that have a Utility title and have acquired a specified number of points and first places in Obedience competition.

positive stress - manifests itself in the dog becoming more active, at the verge of being out of control.

premium list - an announcement for a conformation show and/or Obedience trial that contains the form required to enter a dog as well as the list of judges.

professional handler - someone who handles a dog for and on behalf of the owner.

Pure-Bred Dogs, The American Kennel Gazette - the official monthly publication of the American Kennel Club.

random reward - a reward given in an unpredictable order to obtain the desired response.

separation anxiety - anxiety experienced by the dog when separated from the owner.

stifle - the joint between the upper and second thigh; corresponds to the human knee joint.

stress - *see* **negative stress** *or* **positive stress**.

TD - Tracking Dog. A title awarded by the AKC to dogs that have passed an AKC Tracking test.

TDX - Tracking Dog Excellent. A title awarded by the AKC to dogs that have passed an AKC Tracking Dog Excellent test.

Title - awarded by the AKC for achievements in Obedience or conformation exhibiting.

UD - Utility Dog. An Obedience title awarded by the AKC to dogs that have qualified in three Utility classes. Dogs must have earned a CDX to enter the Utility class. The exercises are the Signal Exercise, Scent Discrimination, Directed Retrieve, Moving Stand and Examination and Directed Jumping.

Utility class - *see* **UD**.

Water Dog (WD) - a water rescue title awarded by the Newfoundland Club of America.

withers - the highest part of the scapula (shoulder blade) at the base of the neck; where the shoulder blades meet.

References for the Motivational Method

Volhard, Jack, and Melissa Bartlett. *What All Good Dogs Should Know: The Sensible Way to Train*. New York: Howell Book House, 1991.

Volhard, Jack and Wendy. *Foundation Training: Level I*. Durham: Green Light Creations, 1988. Videotape.

Volhard, Jack and Wendy. *Motivational Retrieve: Teaching, Practicing, Testing*. New York: Top Dog Training School, 1991. Videotape.

Volhard, Jack and Wendy. *Open and Utility Training: The Motivational Method*. New York: Howell Book House, 1992.

Volhard, Jack and Wendy. *Open Training: The Teaching Phase*. New York: Top Dog Training School, 1990. Videotape.

Volhard, Jack and Wendy. *The Red Book: Lesson Plans & Homework Sheets for Puppies & Beginners, Intermediate & Novice* (8 weeks each). New York: Top Dog Training School, 1994.

Volhard, Jack and Wendy. *Utility Training: The Teaching Phase*. New York: Top Dog Training School, 1990. Videotape.

Volhard, Joachim J., and G. T. Fisher. *Teaching Dog Obedience Classes: The Manual for Instructors*. New York: Howell Book House, 1986.

Volhard, Joachim J., and G. T. Fisher. *Training Your Dog: The Step-by-Step Manual*. New York: Howell Book House, 1983.

Volhard, Wendy. *Back to Basics: A Guide to a Balanced Home-made Dog Food*. New York: Top Dog Training School, 1988.

Publications available from:

Top Dog Training School
R.D. 1, Box 518
Phoenix, NY 13135

Bibliography

Bergman, Goran. *Why Does Your Dog Do That?* New York: Howell Book House, 1973.

Campbell, William E. *Owner's Guide to Better Behavior in Dogs and Cats.* Alpine Publications, 1986.

Carlson, DVM, Delbert G., and James Giffin, MD. *Dog Owner's Home Veterinary Handbook.* New York: Howell Book House, 1992.

Lorenz, Konrad. *Man Meets Dog.* New York: Penguin Books, 1964.

Lorenz, Konrad. *On Aggression.* New York: Harcourt, Brace & World, Inc., 1966.

Most, Konrad. *Training Dogs.* N.p.: Popular Dogs, 1954.

Pfaffenberger, Clarence J. *The New Knowledge of Dog Behavior.* New York: Howell Book House, 1963.

Pryor, Karen. *Lads Before the Wind.* New York: Harper & Row, 1975.

Volhard, Jack, and Melissa Bartlett. *What All Good Dogs Should Know: The Sensible Way to Train.* New York: Howell Book House, 1991.

Volhard, Jack and Wendy. *Open and Utility Training: The Motivational Method.* New York: Howell Book House, 1992.

Volhard, Joachim J., and G. T. Fisher. *Training Your Dog: The Step-by-Step Manual.* New York: Howell Book House, 1983.

Index

155